W9-AHE-604

LOVE & HATE
The Story of Henri Landwirth

BY BILL HALAMANDARIS

TABLE OF CONTENTS

"I have spent a lifetime wondering why the Nazis did what they did. I don't think it is so important anymore to understand why the Nazis wanted to kill all Jews. It is more important to realize that such hatred exists. It is still out there."

...HENRI LANDWIRTH

DREAMS AND NIGHTMARES

March 7, 2006, Founders Day at Give Kids the World. It's Give Kids the World's twentieth anniversary, and Henri Landwirth's 79th birthday. Started in a closet in response to a single wish, Give Kids the World has grown to welcome 75,000 families with sick children. They have come from every state in the union and 50 foreign nations and are now arriving at the pace of 6,000 families a year.

Albert Einstein said, "There are only two ways to live your life.
"One is as though nothing is a miracle. The other is as though every-thing is a miracle."

At Give Kids the World, there is no doubt. Miracles are every-where, abundantly evident. It is a resort like no other, more than 70 acres filled with every form of entertainment for children known to man.

Characters from Orlando's theme parks rarely seen together roam the streets of Kids Village on a regular basis. Today, Goofy, Shamu, Snow White, Barney and Sponge Bob are joined by stilt-walkers, jugglers, clowns and a 16-foot gingerbread man in entertaining the children, their families, and invited guests — executives from Universal, Disney World, Sea World, and Nickelodeon, former as-tronauts, Henri's business partners and friends.

The gingerbread man, specially made by Universal for the occasion, weighs more than 600 pounds. He smiles broadly, seeming to enjoy the sight of children playing the world's largest game of Candyland and riding the carousel at the Castle of Miracles.

A Gingerbread House flanked by two Cup Cake parlors stands next to the Castle of Miracles. Down the Avenue of Angels is Amberville train station, named in honor of one of the Village's special guests. Along the way there is Julie's Safari Theater and an ice cream parlor stocked with all the ice cream a kid can eat. On the other side of the Village there is a water park; Marc's Dino-Putt miniature golf course, with animatronic dinosaurs, water hazards, and fog effects; and a private fishing pond where a kid is guaranteed to catch a fish within 15 minutes.

It is a fairy tale come true, created for terminally ill children, and run by a small staff with the help of 5,000 part-time angels. It is a dream built on a nightmare.

For Henri Landwirth, the nightmare began when he was 13 years old.

INTRODUCTION

"The search after the great man," Emerson wrote, "is the dream of youth and the most serious occupation of manhood." True to Emerson's words, my search for greatness began at an early age when as a boy I was encouraged to read the biographies of great men and women. There I began to consider the measure of greatness, the meaning and purpose of life.

This incipient interest grew into a passion that has dictated the direction of my life. It led me from a small mining town in Utah to the capital of our country, from an initial interest in law to a life of charity, from a career at the U. S. Senate to the establishment of the Caring Institute with my brother, Val, and, finally, beyond that to the creation of The Heart of America Foundation.

These two organizations were founded with many noble objectives and one highly personal purpose – to find, be near, and learn from the most successful human beings on the planet. With that determination, a magnificent odyssey began.

In 1988 as part of this quest, I traveled from Washington, DC to Orlando, Florida to meet Henri Landwirth. It was three years after we began our search and the first year the National Caring Awards would be presented. A quarter of a million people in positions of visibility – Senators, Congressmen, Governors, Mayors, business leaders and members of the media—had been asked to nominate the most caring person they knew. From the thousands nominated, we were now down to a few.

Henri was one of these. After two years of research, I thought I knew him pretty well: He was one of the youngest survivors of the Holocaust. Separated from his family while still a boy, he had spent five years in the closest thing to hell humans can contrive, surviving five different camps before finding freedom. Henri had grown up in a world without kindness, yet the love of life this unkindness kindled inspired everyone we talked to and seemingly everyone he knew.

Henri had lived the American Dream, coming to the United States with nothing but $20 in his pocket and making a fortune in the hotel business. His charitable work had grown geometrically with his success. With the creation of the Fanny Landwirth Foundation, named in memory of the mother he had lost in the Holocaust, he began a determined effort to give something back. His community involvement increased when his friendship with the Mercury 7 astronauts inspired him to start a scholarship foundation that would honor their achievements and extend their example. Now with the creation of Give Kids the World, his charitable instincts had grown to animate and consume his life.

Even knowing all this, I was still unprepared for the man I met. He was about my size – 5' 10" or 11" – yet his presence seemed to fill the room. He spoke with a European accent and occasionally fractured English that only added to his considerable charm. He was immediately engaging, laughing often and effortlessly. When he talked about Give Kids the World, he spoke with the enthusiasm and innocence of the child he never was as if the child within him was finally being allowed to emerge. Every now and then when he talked about the Village he was building for the children, he giggled, releasing an unexpected and surprisingly unrestrained sound of true delight.

The warmth of his personality reached out and enveloped me. I felt a connection on a level I cannot explain. It was as though I had found another piece of myself, a brother I had never known.

Two years earlier, I met Viktor Frankl. Frankl, also a survivor of the holocaust, was then 83 years old, twenty-five years Henri's senior. Credited with making the greatest contribution to psychotherapy since Freud, he was world renown as the founder of Logotherapy; but to most of America, he was known simply as the author of Man's Search for Meaning, *named by the Library of*

Congress as one of the ten most influential books of the 20th Century.

After reading **Man's Search for Meaning,** *I had sent Dr. Frankl a letter expressing my admiration. I told him I had stumbled on his book after an extensive period of soul-searching and that I wished I had found it earlier. This book had a profound impact on me and I told him so.*

To my surprise, Dr. Frankl answered my letter with a personal note raising questions that encouraged a response. We exchanged letters several times after that before I found an opportunity to invite him to come to America to keynote a conference I was helping to organize.

I met Viktor at Washington National Airport late one afternoon in 1986. I peppered him with questions as we drove to town. I continued my questioning over dinner and then reluctantly said goodnight.

The next morning, Viktor gave a stirring and thought provoking speech, receiving a standing ovation from the three thousand people attending the conference. As I went to the dais to escort him to a reception in his honor, he scribbled something on his notes and then handed them to me. When I looked at what he had given me, I found he had autographed the text of his speech and inscribed it with a personal note.

After lunch, I walked him back to his room and thanked him for making the long journey from Vienna for one speech. I said good-bye not knowing when, if ever, I would see him again.

Early the next morning, the phone rang at my home. When I

answered, I heard Viktor's voice. He said his return flight did not leave until late in the day and he was wondering if I would mind coming down and spending some time with him.

We spent the entire day together. Though nothing explicit was said, I could tell he was "working on me." Viktor had clearly thought about the questions I had asked the day he arrived and was trying to extend my thinking. He probed and pushed with the gentle, thoughtful persistence of the good psychiatrist he was.

Afterwards, Viktor periodically sent me the text of something he was working on — a speech or an article — and asked what I thought. His questions were always phrased as though he was seeking my opinion, but I came to know it was just one more way of extending our dialogue.

In much the same manner, I came to expect a periodic phone call. The ones I liked best were the ones where he said he was going to be somewhere in the United States and wondering if I could I find time to join him.

One of the last things Viktor sent me to review contained a portion of a chapter he was preparing for his autobiography. There was little Viktor left to chance and I expect there was no chance in this.

The text described his relationship with Freud. As a young man dreaming of being a psychiatrist, Frankl said he was so eager to meet Freud that he staked out a park in Vienna that Freud was said to frequent, hoping to see him.

Finally, Frankl's effort was blessed with success and he was bold enough to make an approach. He described Freud as gracious, patient, and generous. At the conclusion of their conversation Freud was kind enough to invite Frankl to send him some of his work to review.

"Before long," Viktor wrote, "I was corresponding with Freud on a regular basis, sending him anything I thought would interest him. He promptly answered every letter and was responsible for publishing my first treatise on psychotherapy."

※

When I met Henri, Frankl immediately came to mind. I had the intuitive sense that one had prepared me for the other. In Frankl, I was given a mentor and teacher. In Henri, I knew I had found the best illustration of Frankl's philosophy I would ever encounter.

Strangely, though both men had survived Auschwitz they had never met. Frankl entered the death camps as an adult with two degrees—a doctor of medicine and Ph. D. He was fully formed with his treatise for Logotherapy in hand. Henri was barely more than a child with a sixth grade education. Frankl had entered the concentration camps almost voluntarily, refusing a visa and the promise of safety in America in order to be with his family, while Henri had been torn from his family and sent to a work camp at the age of thirteen.

Frankl returned to Vienna after the war. Henri could hardly wait to leave Europe and get to America. Frankl found validation for his theories and beliefs in Hitler's concentration camps. The same experience largely shaped Henri's view of life.

It was no coincidence, I believed, that these two men entered my life at about the same time. Frankl taught the essence of life was choice, our "response ability." You could not know Henri without marveling at his response to the questions life had handed him and the choices he had made.

Henri had lived in hell. He had seen the worst humanity had to offer and yet he chose to answer with the best. Where there was abundant reason for anger, hate, and bitterness there was only love, forgiveness, joy, and – yes – gratitude.

How was this possible? I wondered. How do you get from hell to humanity? How do you get love from hate? I would spend 20 years trying to answer these questions.

CHAPTER ONE

The sad truth is that most evil is done by people

who never make up their minds

to be either good or evil.

...HANNAH ARENDT

Henri was born in Antwerp, Belgium on March 7, 1927. His twin sister, Margot, followed five minutes later.

Max and Fanny, their parents, had married young. She was seventeen. He was 16 years older. They seemed perfectly suited to each other. Max was soft-spoken, kind and gentle. Fanny was bright and very strict. There was no doubt she was the boss of the house.

Max sold men's clothing and traveled a great deal; but when he was home, Henri remembers, his parents were always together, smiling and laughing, enjoying each other's company, going out together and dancing until late evening.

While he was still an infant, Henri's family moved to Poland where his father had been born. The Nazi Party was founded later that same year. Two years earlier a third element that would prove to be a significant force in Henri's life had began to build with the formation of the German Society for Space Travel. No one could have predicted how these three seemingly unrelated events would coalesce to dictate the direction of Henri's life.

Wernher Von Braun was the son of a Prussian Baron. He was born in Wirsitz, Germany in 1912. His interest in the stars began when he was given a small telescope as a confirmation gift. A year later, he saw an ad in an astronomy magazine for a book called, 'The Rocket to the Interplanetary Spaces,' by Hermann Oberth. Von Braun sent for the book immediately and soon became obsessed by the subject.

"To be an engineer and build a space ship," he quickly decided, "would be a challenge worth living for."

Von Braun became the youngest member of the German Society for Space Travel. By the age of eighteen, he had already begun his life's work as one of Professor Oberth's assistants, working to prove Oberth's theory that liquid rather than solid fuels were the best source of rocket power for space travel.

By the summer of 1932, Von Braun and Oberth had achieved enough success to attract the attention of the German Army. Von Braun saw their interest as an opportunity. Knowing the kind of tests necessary to further his research would, as he later said, "be costly beyond private means," Von Braun joined the German Army's rocket research program. The German Army agreed to sponsor his research and allow him to conduct his experiments at the Kummersdorf Army Proving Ground.

Von Braun made his "deal with the devil" without any apparent regret. "In 1932, the idea of war seemed to us an absurdity," he said in 1950. "The Nazi's weren't even in power. We felt no moral scruples about the possible future abuse of our brainchild. We were interested solely in exploring outer space. It was simply a question with us of how the golden cow could be milked most successfully."

On January 30, 1933, Adolf Hitler became German Reich Chancellor. The first concentration camp, Dachau, near Munich, was established thirty-three days later. Its first inmates were political opponents of the new regime.

Two months later on April 1, 1933, the Nazis initiated a national boycott of Jewish shops and businesses. The following month, books written by Jewish authors were burned. Then, on the 14 of July, legislation was adopted allowing the forced sterilization of Jews, gypsies, afro-Germans, the handicapped, and others considered "below the level of the Aryan race."

In 1936, Jews were told they could only leave Germany under special circumstances and the concentration camp of Buchenwald was established. The following year, Jews were required to carry identity papers at all times, take a middle name identifying them as Jews – 'Israel' for men and 'Sarah' for women – and have their passports stamped with a red 'J'.

Two years later, on March 15, 1939, Germany invaded Czechoslovakia. An invasion of Poland followed on the 1st of September. With that, World War II became a reality. Almost immediately, on the 21 of September, a fiat was issued ordering all Jews in Poland and Czechoslovakia be gathered and placed in ghettos. Next, all Jewish males in Poland between the ages of 14 and 60 were conscripted for forced labor.

"They came to our house," Henri remembers. "They gave us a few hours to get ready and told us the only things we could take with us was whatever we could carry. We were herded like animals into the poorest and dirtiest sections of Krakow where they built a ten-foot wall around us. We could not do anything except stay there. It was extremely difficult."

The ghetto at Krakow, one of five main ghettos created by the Nazis during their occupation of Poland, was a staging point to begin dividing "able workers" from those who would later be deemed worthy only of death. Before the war, nearly 70,000 Jews lived in and around Krakow. It was one of the largest Jewish communities in Poland. Only 15,000 workers and their families were permitted to stay. All other Jews were ordered out of the city, and resettled in surrounding communities.

There were 30 streets and 320 houses in the Krakow ghetto with a total of 3,167 rooms. Before the war, 3,000 people lived in an area now forced to accommodate more than five times that number.

A minimum of four families had to share one flat. It was not uncommon for 10 to 12 people to share a single room. The area was so overcrowded, many people had to live on the streets.

The Nazis ordered all synagogues closed and established a Judenrat—a Jewish governing council for the ghetto. Members of the Judenrat were appointed by the SS, the Nazi party's political police. Created in 1925 to provide personal security for Hitler, the SS grew under the direction of Heinrich Himmler from a small paramilitary organization with less than 300 members to become one the largest and most powerful organizations in Nazi Germany. The Nazis regarded the SS as an elite unit, the party's "Praetorian Guard," with all SS personnel selected on the principles of racial purity and unconditional loyalty to the Nazi Party.

The SS told the Judenrat to fulfill all German orders with absolute obedience and accuracy. One of their first orders was to gather and deliver all of the Jews' personal valuables and historical artifacts from Krakow's synagogues.

"I was upstairs the first time they came," Henri recalls. "They went through the house looking for valuables. I stood beside my father when a German soldier put a gun to his head. The soldier held the barrel of his pistol against my father's temple and demanded to know where we kept our jewelry, furs – anything of value. If we didn't answer, he said my father would be shot."

Henri has forgotten many things, some by choice, some by chance, but he has never able to forget that moment.

Max survived this incident but his reprieve was short-lived. The Nazis took him to a prison called Radom a few months later. He was held there without a trial. Though Fanny daily implored the SS to see her husband and asked for his release, no visitors were allowed. No charges were filed against him but one morning without ceremony or notice, he was marched to the killing fields along with a number of other prisoners. A soldier stood behind each prisoner pointing a rifle at the back of their head. On command, the trigger was pulled and Henri's father joined the others in an unmarked grave.

"The day of my father's arrest is vivid, painted on my memory like photograph," Henri recalls. "It was this single event, more than any other, which changed my perspective on what was happening around me. To lose our home, our possessions, all connection to material things, was terrible, but it was bearable. But to lose each other, to have the foundation of our family shattered simply because we had been born as Jews was an unbelievable sadness that words cannot convey."

As Henri approached his thirteenth birthday, his mother insisted that a bar mitzvah be held for him. He was taken into a cellar with ten men who would help complete the ceremony. Two men stood nearby watching for the police. If they were caught, they knew they would be shot and killed on the spot but that risk didn't matter. Henri would not deny his heritage.

Shortly thereafter, they came for Henri. Though he was only thirteen, he was taken to join those forced into labor. For some reason he had told them he was born in 1926 and therefore a year older than he actually was. Call it a quirk of fate, a bureaucratic blunder, an act of deliberate deception or miracle in the making, this mistake, Henri now believes, kept him alive.

CHAPTER TWO

"Everything that happens to us leaves some trace behind.

Everything contributes imperceptibly to make us what we are."

....JOHANN WOLFGANG VON GOETHE

If it were not for the success of the Stephen Spielberg's film *Schindler's List*, the camp of Plaszow might never have become known to the average American. Because of its popularity every school child knows about this otherwise unremarkable camp and the remarkable cruelty of its Commandant, Amon Goeth.

Plaszow was originally designed as a work camp. However, like many other Nazi camps, prisoners there were starved, worked to death, or shot for no reason. As *Schindler's List* explains, executions in concentration camps had to be approved by the central office in Berlin. There was no such restraint on the will or the whim of those in control of the labor camps.

Plaszow was located south of Krakow near a quarry where prisoners were forced to work as punishment. It grew to cover more than 200 acres, circled by two electric, barbed wire fences separated by a ditch filled with water. Thirteen guard towers manned by the SS with searchlights and machine guns were perched around the perimeter.

Prisoners at Plaszow worked 12-hour shifts. Their daily food ratio was 200 grams of bread or hot water soup.

Henri was employed as a "turner" or carpenter's assistant, helping to build the barracks the camp's burgeoning population required. There were 2,000 prisoners in Plaszow when he arrived, 24,000 when he left.

The camps, started as a way of isolating and controlling those the Nazis found undesirable, became increasingly important to the German economy as the war progressed. There was no way to support the enormous economic effort the war required without forced or slave labor. Soon the law enacted in 1939 requiring all Jewish men to work was expanded to include Jewish women and children as well.

"I don't remember the exact date I was sent from the ghetto to a labor camp," Henri says, "but I will never forget the horrible conditions on the deportation train."

Passengers had been separated by sex. Henri and all the other men were sent to the left, Margot, his mother, and the other women were sent to the right. They were packed in boxcars designed to transport cattle.

"I'm not sure how many people were packed into a single car," Henri recalls, "perhaps as many as one hundred, but there was only room to stand. We had no food or water or bathroom facilities. There was no room and little air. Many people were sick and did not survive. For those of us who survived, it was a gruesome experience."

Even now, Henri's voice becomes animated and his face flashes with anger when it talks about it. "You cannot imagine how it was," he says. "The soldiers had complete control and they used it. Our lives had no meaning to them. We were like ants…like bugs. To step on us made no difference."

In the ghetto, Henri remembers a beautiful young woman with short black hair and bright, brown eyes. Bravely, she stood up to a Nazi SS officer. "You cannot treat human beings this way!" she said.

The officer pushed her away. Without a warning or a word, he withdrew his pistol and shot her in the head. She fell dead at his feet. He holstered his weapon and stepped over her like a man stepping over a mud puddle.

One night in Plaszow Henri risked his life to see his mother. He had heard where she might be from one of the other inmates who had been in the women's compound on a work detail. Henri, still a boy, crawled through the wire that separated the two areas and went looking where he was told his mother might be.

Sneaking quietly from one barracks to another, he inquired if his mother was within or if anyone knew where he could find her. Finally, someone told him where she was.

"When I found my mother and I had to tell her who I was." Henri says. "She could hardly recognize me. She said, 'Son, do you have any food I can have?' She was very hungry and I had nothing, not even a piece of bread to give her."

That was the last time Henri saw his mother. She survived until near the end of the war when, Henri later learned, she was herded on to a ship with 2,000 other women. The ship was taken out into the harbor and blown-up, leaving Henri an orphan with only memories of his parent's love.

CHAPTER THREE

"People ask, 'Where was God in the concentration camp?'

He was always just above, watching and

wondering – where is man?"

...VIKTOR FRANKL

World War II marked a transition point for the development of concentration camps: their purpose broadened and evolved, the number of inmates exploded. At the end of 1939, there were only seven concentration camps. By the end of the war, there were 22 concentration camps with 1,200 satellite camps, and thousands of smaller affiliated camps.

The first inmates were political opponents of the Nazi regime. Then the Nazis began targeting 'harmful' elements within the German society—Jews, gypsy, homosexuals, the handicapped and any others considered inferior. With the beginning of the War, the concentration camps began to overflow with thousands of prisoners of war.

As the camp system evolved, so did their purpose. Camp

labor became of enormous economic significance. Every effort was made to maximize the benefit and minimize the cost. Those unable to work had always been weeded out; now this process was organized with machine like precision. People who were unproductive were dispatched immediately. Those who could work were "worked to death." There were plenty of prisoners to take their place. The death rate in Dachau, for example, increased from 4% in 1938 to 36% in 1942. The death rate at Mauthausen increased from 24% in 1939 to 76% in 1940.

The systematic killing of Jews began with mobile killing squads called Einsatzgruppen. Each group consisted of four units of 500-900 men. Fifty years later, Hans Friedrich, one of the Nazis involved in this process described his work to an American journalist working for PBS:

Friederich: Try to imagine there is a ditch, with people on one side, and behind them soldiers. That was us and we were shooting. And those who were hit fell down into the ditch...They were so utterly shocked and frightened, you could do with them what you wanted.

Journalist: Could you tell me what you were thinking and feeling when you were shooting?

Friederich: Nothing. I only thought, 'Aim carefully' so that you hit properly. That was my thought.

Journalist: This was your only thought? During all that time you had no feelings for the people, the Jewish civilians that you shot.

Friederich: No.

Journalist: And why not?

Friederich: Because my hatred towards the Jews is too great...And I admit my thinking on this point is unjust. I admit this. But what I experienced from my earliest youth when I was living on a farm, what the Jews were doing to us—well that will never change. That is my unshakable conviction.

Journalist: What in God's name did the people you shot have to do with those people who supposedly treated you badly at home?

Friederich: Nothing, but to us they were Jews.

By the time Himmler ordered a halt to these efforts in the fall of 1942, the Nazi killing squads had murdered more than one and a half million Jews. Ironically, Himmler's stop order was based on a sympathetic reaction – not for the victims but for their executioners. He thought a less personal way of killing Jews would spare his soldiers emotional anguish.

With that, the development of extermination camps began. In these camps, there was no work alternative or selection process. Jews and other "undesirables" were simply destroyed upon arrival. It was Hitler's "final solution to Jewish questions." Gassing vans, freezing showers, and other creative measures were used until the death camps could become fully operational.

In all, World War II killed some 28 million Europeans. Hitler's death squads killed at least 20 million more. The Nazis killed one out of every six Polish or Soviet citizens under their rule. Included in this total are several million children.

"Why the children," a member of the killing squad was asked.

"The children, they are not the enemy at the moment," he responded. "The enemy is the blood inside them. The enemy is the growing up to be a Jew that could be dangerous. And because of that the children were included as well."

Henri's journey through the camps followed the path of their development, from bad to worse to worst: Plaszow to Radom, Radom to Auschwitz, Auschwitz to Mauthausen, Mauthausen to Gusen, Gusen to Flossenberg, Flossenberg to a place with no name where he was confined underground for what seemed an eternity. Each move took Henri deeper into Germany territory. Each new camp put him in place where his chances of survival were reduced.

"The probability of survival in Auschwitz was 1 to 29," Viktor told me, "as can be statistically evidenced. Ninety percent of the people on our transport were killed within a few hours of their arrival."

If that is true, the odds of Henri's survival are beyond comprehension.

Germany invaded Demark, Norway, Belgium, the Netherlands, and France in the spring of 1940. The invasion of Greece and Yugoslavia followed a year later. Hundreds of thousands of Jews, gypsies, and other undesirables were sent from captured territories to the extermination camps.

Meanwhile, the Nazis were testing their ultimate weapon, the V-2 rocket developed by Wernher von Braun's research team. The V-2 rocket stood 46 feet 11 inches tall, and 5 feet 5 inches in diameter. It weighed 14 tons at takeoff and carried a 2,000 pound warhead.

The first rocket was launched in 1942. It traveled less than a mile before falling back. Subsequent tests later that year extended its range from 5 miles to 118. With this success, the project attracted Himmler's interest. He took control of the project personally, rewarding von Braun by giving him the rank of an officer in the SS.

CHAPTER FOUR

"It is by those who have suffered

that the world is advanced."

...LEO TOLSTOY

"I arrived with fifteen hundred other people," Frankl wrote in *Man's Search for Meaning*. "We had been traveling by train for several days and nights. There were eighty people in each coach. The carriages were so full that only the top parts of the windows were free to let in the grey dawn. Everyone expected the train to head for some munitions factory, where we would be employed as forced labor. We did not know whether we were still in Silesia or already in Poland. The engine's whistle had an uncanny sound, like a cry for help sent out in commiseration for the unhappy load it was destined to lead to perdition. Then the train shunted, obviously nearing a main station. Suddenly a cry broke out from the ranks of the anxious passengers, "There is a sign, Auschwitz!" Everyone's heart missed a beat at that moment. Auschwitz – the very name stood for all that was horrible: gas chambers, crematoriums, and massacres. Slowly, *almost hesitatingly, the train moved on as if it wanted to spare its passengers the dreadful realization as long as possible: Auschwitz!"*

"Auschwitz" has become synonymous with genocide and the Holocaust. It is the site of the single largest mass murder in the history of humanity.

Auschwitz is located about 60 miles south of Krakow. Near a major railroad line in an area with abundant natural resources – particularly fresh water, lime, and coal—it was an ideal site for IG Farben, the German industrial conglomerate, to build a factory that would manufacture war materials.

Himmler saw it an opportunity to create a model Nazi settlement. Prisoners from Auschwitz would work as slave laborers. The SS would profit from selling their labor, as well as, the coal and gravel they produced.

Near the end of 1940, Himmler visited Auschwitz. Pleased by what he saw, he ordered the camp be tripled in capacity. Auschwitz went from a small backwater to the largest camp in the Nazi empire.

Under Himmler's orders, the Euthanasia Program, established initially to purify the Aryan race by eliminating mentally and physically disabled Germans, was extended to the concentration camps, eliminating the need to transport, house, and feed people who could not work. Adolf Eichmann suggested using "showers" of carbon monoxide for this purpose. He pointed out this had been done successfully with mental patients in some places under the Reich's control. The Nazi's experimented with this process, "Hell Vans", freezing showers, and a number of other approaches before settling on Zyklon B. Zyklon B was a pesticide used to kill lice in prisoner's clothing. Once exposed to heated air, the crystals produced a lethal gas. It was cheap and readily available.

By the time Henri arrived, the four crematoria at Auschwitz were fully operational. They housed eight gas chambers and 46 ovens that could dispose of 4,400 corpses per day.

⚜

"I inquired from prisoners who had been there some time where my colleague and friend had been sent," Frankl said.

"Was he sent to the left side?"

"Yes, I replied."

"Then you can see him there, I was told."

"Where?"

"A hand pointed to the chimney a few hundred yards off, which

was sending a column of flame up into the grey sky of Poland. As I watched, it dissolved into a sinister cloud of smoke."

"My barrack was right next to where they had the showers," Henri recalls. "It was a terrible thing to stay in that barrack next to where they were burning people. But we had no choice. The smoke smelt terribly. And they were going around the clock. Night and day."

"Auschwitz was my first realization that the camps were there for our extermination. I never expected to get out of there. I knew it would be a matter of time and I would be murdered like the rest. The smoke of the dead was so thick it filled my throat. I thought I would go crazy. I wanted to tear my heart out and stop living that very second. I felt powerless to help myself and worse, powerless to help those I loved."

Frankl was awakened one night from a deep sleep by the groans of another prisoner. The man threw himself about and called out, obviously having a horrible nightmare. Instinctively, Viktor started to wake the poor man then stopped short, appalled at himself.

"I drew back the hand which was ready to shake him frightened at the thing I was about to do," Frankl said. *"At that moment I became intensely conscious of the fact that no dream, no matter how horrible, could be as bad as the reality of the camp which surrounded us, and to which I was about to recall him."*

For Henri, *Auschwitz* was the nightmare. "I sometimes looked to God for a miracle," he said, "but I saw no sign that miracles existed in Auschwitz, only nightmares come awake. At least that's what I thought before my eyes learned to see that there were miracles all around me."

Now that his eyes have been opened Henri sees miracles in his past as well as his present. When he arrived at Auschwitz, for example, he had a chronic skin disease call psoriasis. It was a long-standing condition that left blemishes on his face, neck and arms. Little did he know that alone should have been his death sentence. In addition, Henri's odds of survival were diminished by the fact that he was a twin.

Dr. Josef Mengele arrived at Auschwitz a year before Henri. An SS physician, Mengele saw Auschwitz as his personal laboratory, one that allowed him to experiment on women, children, infants and others as he pleased. He took particular delight in experimenting on twins, injecting chemicals into their eyes in an attempt to change eye color, stitching twins together, and removing limbs and organs without using an anesthetic.

A survivor of one of Mengele's experiments described her experience this way: "Mengele came in every morning after roll call to count us. He wanted to know every morning how many guinea pigs he had. Three times a week they took blood from my left arm. At the same time they would give me a minimum of five injections into my right arm. After one of these injections, I became extremely ill. Mengele came in the next morning with four other doctors. He looked at my fever chart and said, laughing sarcastically, 'Too bad, she is so young. She has only two weeks to live.' I faded in and out of consciousness, but I kept telling myself: I must survive. I must survive. If I had died, my twin sister Miriam would have been rushed immediately to Mengele's lab and killed with an injection to the heart so that Mengele could do comparative autopsies. This is the way most of the twins died."

Polished boots slightly apart, his thumb resting on his pistol belt, Mengele's surveyed his prey as they arrived. With a flick of a cane clasped in a gloved hand, he determined death or life. A gesture to the left meant death; a gesture to the right meant life as Frankl had painfully learned.

As if by magic, Henri's skin condition cleared up before it could be detected. If it hadn't, he surely would have joined those sent to the left. His psoriasis would not return until he was free. Because he had lied about his age, telling the Nazis he was a year older than he was, the closeness of his relationship with his sister, Margot, was also not apparent. The twins had been separated before going to Plaszow. She would not arrive in Auschwitz until the day he left.

"There is a night in Auschwitz I particularly remember," Henri said half a century later. "I was watching the crematoriums. You could smell the human skin burning. The stench was terrible. A sick smell worse than you can describe. It was a putrid, hellish smell. I saw people lining up to go to their deaths. I couldn't take my eyes from this scene. It was so crazy it didn't seem like it could actually be taking place."

"While I watched one woman tried to resist. She grabbed a gun from an SS man and tried to kill him. She was so brave. He took the gun away from her and shot her in the heart. She died on the spot. The guards picked her up and carried her over to the crematoriums like she was a piece of wood for a fire."

The other vivid memory Henri still carries is constant and enduring hunger. "To be hungry, really, deathly hungry, to ache for food is the worst torture anyone can imagine," he says. "It has a way of focusing all of a person's energy on himself. It's hard to think of your neighbor's pain when it feels like a wild animal inside your stomach is eating you from the inside out. To be thirsty is even worse. I was hungry and thirsty for more than five years. Real hunger and thirst reduces man to the level of animals. I thought about food all the time."

"Those who have not gone through a similar experience can hardly conceive of the soul-destroying mental conflict and clashes of will power which a famished man experiences," Frankl said. "They can hardly grasp what it means to stand digging in a trench, listening only for the siren to announce 9:30 or 10:00 AM – the half-hour lunch interval – when bread would be rationed out (as long as it was still available); repeatedly asking the foreman – if he wasn't a disagreeable fellow – what the time was; and tenderly touching a piece of bread in one's coat pocket, first stroking it with frozen gloveless fingers, then breaking off a crumb and putting it in one's mouth and finally, with the last bit of will power, pocketing it again, having promised oneself that morning to hold off till afternoon."

The impact days of hunger approaching starvation had on his body became apparent one day after Henri had been at Auschwitz for a while. "We were standing in line naked and I looked at the back of the man in front of me," he says. "I was shocked at how clearly I could see his skeleton through his skin. I remember how his backbone was divided into inch long little circles stacked on top of each other. His rib bones reminded me of a barrel without a lid. His shoulder blades stood out. As I looked at him I realized the man behind me was seeing the same thing I was."

"A man counted only because he had a prison number, Viktor said. "One literally became a number: dead or alive – that was unimportant; the life of a "number" was completely irrelevant. What stood behind the number and that life mattered even less. The fate, the history, the name of the man was nothing."

Henri Landwirth became B4343.

CHAPTER FIVE

"The course of human history is determined

not by what happens in the skies but

what takes place in our hearts."

...SIR ARTHUR KEITH

In January 1945, the Nazis began to evacuate Auschwitz. The allies had landed at Normandy six months before and the tide of war had turned against them. Viktor was loaded on a train for transport to an unknown destination.

"We became more and more tense as we approached a bridge we knew the train would have to cross to reach Mauthausen," he said. "You cannot possibly image the dance of joy performed in the cattle car by the prisoners when they saw our transport was not crossing the bridge and was instead 'only' going to Dachau."

Mauthausen was known as the "Hell of Hells." Initially, it was established to provide slave labor for the Wiener Graben stone quarry. A single campsite located near the villages of Mauthasen and Gusen expanded to become one of the largest labor complexes under Nazi control. Ultimately, there were four main camps at Mauthausen and nearby Gusen and more than 50 sub camps.

The first inmates at Mauthausen were hardened criminals and others considered "dangerous to the Third Reich." Mauthausen carried the designation of a Category III camp. It was the only Category III camp in the Nazi's concentration camp system.

The Category III designation meant Mauthausen was a camp of "no return." It was the equivalent of death row in a maximum-security prison, only death row as we know it would seem humane by comparison. Mauthausen was designed to make what little was left of prisoners lives as painful and unpleasant as possible.

As the war progressed, Mauthausen's purpose expanded. It became a significant source of labor for the German war machine. The caves around Gusen were a natural location for an armaments industry forced to go underground by the allies' attacks.

Supporting the war effort at Mauthausen-Gusen became so important that at the height of its capacity Mauthausen had more than 500,000 square meters of bombproof production area. Mauthausen supplied 200 tons of gravel per day, produced ten percent of all German rifles, and thirty-five percent of all Messerschmitt aircraft. In all, labor from Mauthausen supported 43 companies contributing to the Nazi's war effort. It was one of the most profitable concentration camps in the system, providing an annual profit of more than 10 million Reich marks.

The key to Mauthausen's success was its labor supply. At Mauthausen, workers were abundant and expendable. Little was spent for their care and feeding, nothing for their medical care. There was no compensation other than the privilege of remaining alive to work another 12-hour day.

For those not so fortunate, there was a gas chamber at Mauthausen but it was modest in comparison to Auschwitz. It had a maximum capacity of 120. Instead, inmates were subjected to barbaric conditions, the most infamous of which was being forced to carry heavy stone blocks up 186 steps from the base of the quarry. These steps were so fatal they became known as the "Stairway of Death."

Some prisoners were made to jump off the top quarry, a practice the SS with sick humor called "the parachute jump." Others were murdered in railway cars converted into mobile gas chambers, given ice showers or lethal injections, beaten to death or shot, starved, drowned, electrocuted, or hung.

The deathbed confession of the camp commander, Franz Ziereis, shot by American soldiers while trying to escape, is chilling.

"I, myself, am not a wicked man," he said. "I have risen through work."

A merchant by profession Ziereis had joined the army in 1924. He came up through the ranks to the position he held as Commandant of the entire Mauthausen camp complex. Pressed by his interrogators to clear his conscience, he described the number of inmates killed by his subordinates and their manner of death in great detail.

"Altogether, as far as I know," he said, "65,000 inmates were murdered in Mauthausen. In most cases, I myself took part in the executions."

Ziereis concluded by saying he had taught his twelve-year old son to shoot on the rifle range using inmates for targets.

When the man now known as B4343 arrived, the average survival period for prisoners at Mauthausen-Gusen was four months. Henri would last more than nine months before being sent somewhere worse. Still, his memories of Mauthausen, Gusen and Flossenberg are painfully clear, starting with his arrival.

"We were loaded onto cattle cars and transported three days and three nights to Mauthausen," he said. "It was one of the worst experiences I have ever lived through. There was no place to sit, no place to go to the bathroom, and barely room to stand. Finally, at the beginning of the second day, I managed to sit down, and from there I squeezed myself into a cramped laying position.

"When we left Auschwitz, we were given one piece of bread. The Germans said the trip would only take one day, but by then I knew better. I knew they lied. My body was screaming for me to eat the bread but I would not let myself. I could not face the possibility of being on that train without bread. I simply could not. I put the bread under my head and fell asleep. When I woke, the bread was gone. One of my fellow unfortunates had stolen it from me. I wept when I lost my bread."

It was bitter cold when the train arrived at Mauthausen. Many people had not survived the train ride. As they were marched to the camp Henri felt the weather like he had never felt it before.

"I knew I was dying," he said. "I stared at the ground and wondered which step would be my last. My mind was very clear. Death was near and I knew it and welcomed it and had no fear of anything that came with it. How could it be worse than this life?

"I still don't know how I survived. We arrived dressed in rags. There, they took all of our clothes from us. Everything. They stripped us naked and left us in the freezing weather for more than a day. The Germans wanted as many to die by the weather as possible. Many did. The rest of us, they put to work."

By May of 1943, the V-2 rocket was considered operational. More than 100 rockets were successfully fired against military targets in June, causing Hitler to assign the highest priority to the V-2 program.

"This is a measure that can decide the war," Hitler told Albert Speer, "and what encouragement to the home front when we attack the English with it. This is the decisive weapon of the war, and what is more it can be produced with relatively small resources."

Hitler concluded by telling Speer to push development of the rocket as hard as possible.

In 1970, Henri returned to Mauthausen. He wanted his sons, Gary and Greg, to see the camps for themselves. It was a quiet, sober journey.

"My memory moved to the past, when this camp had been my only reality," Henri recalls. "Even in the company of my children, I felt distant and alone. As we went through the barracks, I pointed out things to them like the wooden lofts a few feet above each other where dozens of men slept almost on top of each other. I remembered how it felt to lie on that wood, so close to the others that I wasn't sure if I was touching and smelling myself or them."

The Landwirths were the only ones in the camp on that day. As they prepared to leave, they realized the guard had locked the gate and gone to lunch.

"We couldn't get out of the camp," Henri says. "I cannot tell you how I felt standing with my children behind that locked gate. I became very frightened, very nervous. My heart hurt. I was there with my children and we were locked inside. I thought of my own parents, of what it is like to be with those you love more than life itself, that you would die to protect, and be incapable of saving them."

CHAPTER SIX

"Even the person who seems least important is slowly

being prepared for some special

mission to benefit mankind."

...ALBERT EINSTEIN

Mittelbau-Dora or Mittelbau was formally established in 1944 near Nordhausen, Germany. It was an underground production facility for armaments, notably the V-2 rocket (short for Vergeltungswaff 2 or "Vengeance Weapon 2). When the V-2 was declared operational, labor became the biggest obstacle to quick implementation of the new weapon. Arthur Rudolph, von Braun's chief engineer, learned of the availability of concentration camp prisoners and enthusiastically endorsed their use.

Production of the V-2 rocket was organized along an industrial model assembly line. SS Brigadier General Hans Kammler, who had been in charge of building the extermination camps and gas chambers at Auschwitz-Birkenau, Maidenek, and Belzec, was placed in charge.

The first task was to expand pre-existing tunnels created by gypsum and anhydrite mining. The first prisoners delivered to Mittelbau were assigned this task. Within months, 46 cross tunnels were blasted out of the mountain. The two main tunnels ran parallel to each other, 500 feet apart. They were each a mile and a quarter long, cut completely through the mountain at ground level, and wide enough to accommodate twin railroad tracks.

The prisoners were made to eat and sleep within the tunnels they dug. Thousands of workers were crammed into stinking, lice infested bunks stacked four-high. Blasting was continuous, 24 hours a day. It filled the tunnels with gypsum dust and fumes. There was no running water or sanitary facilities. Dysentery, typhus, tuberculosis and starvation were a constant threat to life. As a result, more people died building the V-2 rocket than the Nazi's were able to kill with it.

B4343 arrived at Mittelbau on February 13, 1945. Henri describes it simply: "It was a worse nightmare than Matthausen and Gusen combined."

He slept on a spring without a mattress. His pillow was his shoes. He didn't get to shower often and soon became infested with fleas.

"Every night I would kill fleas," he says, "until I finally fell asleep."

Henri was very skinny by this point and constantly cold. He lived and worked in the dark. There was no sunlight to warm his bones or give him hope. The experience was so brutal and disorienting that for more than sixty years he thought he had been confined in this place he knew by no name for years instead of months.

Mittelbau had a prisoner resistance organization, which sought mainly to delay production of Hitler's weapons of retaliation, sabotaging the rockets the camp was designed to produce. Shortly after Henri arrived, they contacted him.

"They asked me to misuse a tool, a very precise tool used to measure the size of the part I was making," Henri remembers. "They said if I was off by just a fraction it would be enough to make the weapons useless."

Henri knew what they were asking him to do was dangerous. Prisoners involved in the production of weapons were required to put slips of paper bearing their identification numbers alongside the parts they made or mark the parts they produced so they could be punished if problems were found. The penalty was death.

More than once he had been summoned to watch the SS hang suspected saboteurs. While Henri and the other inmates watched, huge cranes would hoist victims up to the ceiling by ropes tied to their necks. They were left dangling there while they suffocated, choked and strangled. When they were dead, their bodies were lowered and left hanging for days about five feet from the floor, a gruesome reminder to the prisoners who came and went beneath them.

Still, it did not take much convincing to win Henri's cooperation. "They had been trying to kill me for five years," he says. "I was happy to mess things up. The thought that these weapons would be useless made me feel good."

As compensation for the risk they were asking him to take, the resistance told Henri that if he helped them they would help him.

Two weeks or two months later, no one knows for sure, one of Henri's friends came down with typhus. He wasn't dying yet, but he believed, as did the other inmates, that the best way to fight the illness was to not eat.

"He offered me his soup," Henri says. "Even though I knew I would probably catch the disease, I took it anyway. I was so hungry I ate it."

Within days, Henri had typhus. When he couldn't work anymore, he was sent to the camp infirmary to die.

"There were over 25 men dying in that room," Henri recalls.

Henri was put in a corner. The smell of death was in the air. He watched the man next to him die. He heard the sounds of dying people everywhere else in the room before he lost consciousness.

In the middle of the night when Henri was nearly out his mind with fever, someone came to him—an angel dressed in rags.

"Landwirth?" he said.

Fever-ridden and delirious, Henri couldn't see the man who spoke to him. He could barely move but he managed to nod his head.

The visitor bent over and picked up Henri's head. He put a pill in Henri's mouth and gave him a sip of water. Then the angel vanished as quickly as he had appeared.

"When I woke the next morning," Henri says, "almost everyone else was dead."

Henri sat up and looked around. He was in a room full of corpses with a few men still fighting for life.

When the guards came in to haul the bodies to the crematorium, one of them noticed Henri was still alive.

"He looked at me like I was a ghost," Henri says. "Then he ordered me to go back to work."

Mittelbau produced 4,775 V-2 rockets between August l944 and March l945. The first V-2 rocket was launched toward England on September 7, 1944. In the next few months, over 5,000 V-2s were fired on Britain. Only 1,100 reached their target. They killed 2734 people and badly injured another 6,000.

After the war, Von Braun denied ever visiting the Mittelbau concentration camps but others place him on the scene, some say frequently. According to one report, German scientists led by von Braun saw everything that went on.

"When they walked along the corridors, they saw prisoners' drudgery, their exhausting work and their ordeal," a former inmate recalled. "On a little area beside the clinic shack you could see piles of prisoners every day who had not survived the workload or had been tortured to death by vindictive guards...But Prof. Wernher von Braun just walked past them, so close that he almost touched the bodies."

Early in March 1945, the Nazis began to evacuate prisoners from Dora-Mittelbau. Henri had just turned eighteen. First Lady Laura Bush's father, Harold B. Welch, was attached to the infantry division that freed the few remaining prisoners at Dora-Mittelbau a month later.

"He kept that memory the rest of his life," the First Lady said on the sixtieth anniversary of that event, "but he couldn't bear to talk

about it. He couldn't bear to tell his child that there could be such evil in the world."

Call it a twist of fate or the hand of God; the highest technological achievement of the twentieth century was born from this low point of humanity. The seeds planted in the mountains of Germany would blossom twenty years later on the coast of Florida.

CHAPTER SEVEN

"Whenever one life touches another we help or hinder.

There is no escape—man drags

man down or lifts man up."

...BOOKER T. WASHINGTON

The evacuation of Mittelbau was part of the death marches that began in the summer of 1944 and escalated through the end of the war as the Germans lost ground to the advancing armies from the east and the west.

It is estimated a quarter of a million prisoners who had somehow managed to survive years of misery and brutality in the concentration camps, died as liberty approached.

Out of 2,000 people in Henri's unit at Mittelbau, less than 300 hundred were still alive when orders came to leave.

"We were marched for two days and nights away from the front line," Henri remembers.

Crazed by exhaustion and still recovering from his illness,

Henri called out to his friends, telling them to make a run for the woods.

"We can escape," he said. "Let's make a run for it."

Henri had no way of knowing he was being transferred to the camp of last resort – Bergen-Belsen. He only knew he couldn't take it any more. He had reached the breaking point.

Unfortunately, he was overheard by one of his captors. The soldier grabbed his rifle by the barrel and swung it in a full circle like a sledgehammer, smashing Henri's skull.

"I saw the soldier swing the rifle," Henri says. "I knew he was going to hurt me, maybe kill me, but for some reason I didn't move."

He fell to the ground covered with blood. As the soldier turned his attention back to the other prisoners, Henri managed to crawl a few inches. He burrowed into a small pile of straw before he lost consciousness and was left for dead.

When he came to, it was dark. He was alone in a ditch. His head hurt and was covered with blood.

Ironically, as Henri would find out later, rather than kill him the soldier who hit him may have saved his life. Most of the other prisoners evacuated with Henri were executed and buried in a mass grave. Once again he had miraculously escaped his father's fate.

Henri's was alive but his skull was fractured. He felt dizzy and sick to his stomach. He walked a short distance and had to sit down. Before he could walk much further, he was re-captured by a Nazi patrol.

Henri was still thinking about running away when a guard pushed him down a flight of stone steps into a dungeon in a nearby town. He saw water running down the stone walls of his new prison. It was infested with rats, mice and other vermin. Once again he was in a place without light. He put his aching head in his hands and began to cry. He had reached the limit of his endurance.

Three days later, a Nazi opened the cellar door and told him to come out. "I knew he was going to shoot me," Henri says. "I could hear it in his voice. When I looked in his eyes, I could see it in his face."

He ordered Henri to kneel, kiss his hand, and beg for mercy. Henri did what he was told like a man apart. He felt totally numb, a witness watching himself being humiliated from some distant place.

"These things were happening to me, but at the same time they weren't," Henri says. "While I kissed the guard's hand, I thought, 'if you want to shoot me, go ahead and shoot me.'"

Through all the years of the war, this is the face Henri remembers the most. It has become for him the collective face representing all his tormentors – a well-fed soldier, taking delight in humiliating a starving boy. Yet for some reason, perhaps the look in Henri's eye, the soldier changed his mind. He told Henri to get up and run like a dog.

Again, Henri did what he was told to do. He ran as fast as he could but he was soon recaptured. It was as if the Germans were well-fed housecats playing with a frightened mouse. When they tired of their game, they took him to another house on the outskirts of town along with four other prisoners.

By this time, Henri had become fluent in several languages, including German. He heard an officer order his guards to take him and his four new companions to the forest and shoot them.

There was now no doubt. This was the end of wondering. He knew he would die this day. He would die as his father had died, a senseless death from a bullet to the brain.

Strangely, he found he was beyond caring. He walked calmly toward the forest, prepared to accept his fate.

"But then a miracle happened," Henri recalls. Two redeemed the rest.

One of the soldiers, troubled by the fact that he was going to have to shoot Henri and his companions, turned to his comrade and said, "The war is almost over. I don't want to kill these people. Let's just let them go."

To Henri's surprise the other guard agreed.

When they reached the edge of the woods, the guards told

Henri and his four companions to line up facing the woods. "I'm not going to shoot you," one soldier said. "When I raise my gun – run!"

Not sure whether the guard meant what he said, whether it was a gift or a cruel hoax, Henri ran. Without any form of communication the other prisoners instinctively ran in different directions. They ran as though their lives depended on it, fleeing for freedom.

When Henri could not run any more, he walked. Resting as little as possible, he kept moving. He ran and walked aimlessly for days, avoiding all public contact for fear of being recaptured again.

Henri was in terrible physical shape. He was exhausted, delirious, and nearly out of his mind. The gash on his head had become infected. Wounds had developed on his legs. Large holes that were bone-deep had developed in his left leg. The odor of his own rotting flesh followed him as he fled, traveling from village to village, skirting the edge of town and avoiding civilization.

He stole what little food he needed and avoided sight. Each day, the pain in his legs seemed to get more severe. He felt like he was walking on shards of glass. Pus seeped from the holes in his legs. Gangrene infected his body.

Deeper wounds, the wounds five years in the camps had inflicted on his soul, fed on his psyche. It was hard to close his eyes without thinking of the crematoriums. Pain, humiliation and the sounds of suffering played endless in his mind. Rage ripped through him. The more he walked the angrier he became. Images of his parents haunted him. He thought of his father's death and wondered if by some miracle his mother and sister were still alive.

"At this point, I was really crazy," Henri says. "I yelled at the sky and made no sense. I didn't know where I was or where I was going. I only knew I wanted to get as far away from where I was as possible."

When he could walk no longer, Henri found an empty house on the outskirts of a small village. He crawled inside, covered himself with straw, and went to sleep. He awoke to find an old woman standing over him.

To his surprise, she said he crossed the border and was now in Czechoslovakia. The war was over, she said. He didn't have to run anymore.

Henri listened to her, shaking his head in disbelief. Not knowing how else to convince him, she invited him to come and listen to the radio at her home across the street. As he limped over to the woman's window, she went inside the house and turned the radio on.

"When I heard the news," Henri recalls, "I fell to the ground and began to cry."

◢

The German armed forces surrendered unconditionally in the west on May 7. They surrendered on the east two days later. May 8, 1945 was proclaimed Victory in Europe Day (V-E Day).

A month earlier, the Russians had begun attacking the suburbs of Berlin. Hitler spent his 56th birthday, April 20, in his bunker 50 feet underground. He would never see the light of day.

With the outcome of the war no longer in doubt, von Braun assembled his planning staff and asked them to decide to whom they would like to surrender. Afraid of Soviet retaliation for Nazi atrocities on the eastern front, von Braun and his staff quickly decided to try to surrender to the Americans. Hiding key documents in an abandoned mine, von Braun used forged papers to steal a train and lead 500 scientists and engineers through war-torn Germany toward the American lines.

Finally von Braun's party stopped to wait at Haus Ingeborg, a resort hotel on the border of Oberjock, near Austria. While Henri ran and wandered aimlessly from town to town, stealing food and sleeping in barns, von Braun and his friends ate well and slept comfortably. They played cards and listened to the radio.

When they heard the Americans were drawing near, Magnus von Braun, Wernher's brother, was dispatched to make a deal. On May 2, the day after Hitler's death was announced, young Magnus peddled off on a bicycle to meet the Americans. The first soldier he en-

countered was a sentry with the 324th Infantry of the 44th Infantry Division, PFC Frederick Schneikert.

"My name is Magnus von Braun," the rocket scientist said to the army private. "My brother invented the V-2. We want to surrender."

The American command quickly realized the importance of von Braun and his engineers. Troops were dispatched to von Braun's headquarters and Nordhausen to capture the remaining V-2s. Enough components were found to fill 300 hundred train cars for shipment back to the states. The V-2 rocket plans von Braun had hidden were also recovered, but the Russians captured much of Von Braun's production team.

Chapter Eight

"He who has a why to live can bear almost any how."

...FRIEDERICH NIETZSCHE

The old woman called her husband. He came outside and asked Henri if he could carry him inside the house and give him a bath. Henri had not had a bath in months. He was filthy and covered with festering wounds.

The old man picked the eighteen-year old boy up like a sack of feathers. There was no meat and little muscle left on his bones. He took Henri to the bathroom, gently washed his body and cleaned his sores as best he could. It was the first time anyone had touched Henri with kindness in five years.

"I can't tell you what that meant to me," Henri says. "It was the most wonderful thing in the world. It was as this man was saying, I want to replace your bad memories with this gentle one."

When Henri was clean, the couple gave him a bed and brought doctors in to see him. The doctors told Henri his legs were infected with gangrene. They said they would excise the wounds as deeply as possible, but if that didn't work they would have to amputate or the infection would kill him.

Henri still remembers the pain. "It was one of the worst pains I have ever experienced," he says. "They had to burn all the rotting flesh in my legs all the way to the bone."

It was a long and complicated procedure. As they left, one of the doctors told Henri he was lucky the old woman found him when she did. If another hour had passed, there is nothing they could have done.

In another of the miracles that have marked Henri's life, the doctors succeeded in saving his legs. They also drained the infection from his fractured skull and eased his pain. With their help, he once again dodged death.

Within a week Henri was able to stand on his own. When he did, he got a glimpse of himself in a mirror for the first time in five years.

"In the camps we didn't really know how horrible we looked," He recalls. "The only mirror we saw was in the eyes of people who looked the same as we did. When everyone looks the way you do, you think that's normal. As strange as it sounds, I think we all got used to our appearance.

"When I looked into that mirror in Czechoslovakia what I saw was almost beyond my comprehension. I wanted to see myself but at the same time I didn't. I wanted to look away, but I couldn't. My eyes kept staring into that glass. Where my face should have been, I saw little more than skin covering bones. The picture of that face, a face I knew but didn't know, travels with me still."

Am I right in my understanding that your theories had been developed before you went to Auschwitz? I asked Frankl.

"That's correct, he said, "the first version of my book the Doctor and the Soul was hidden in my overcoat when I arrived. Of course, it was immediately destroyed. But I reconstructed the manuscript and the experiences I had in the concentration camps then served as validation of my theories. In truth, I found it is the orientation toward a meaning to fulfill in the future that gave people a chance to survive even this abyss experience. Those people who had a vision of the future in freedom where they could either devote themselves again to a life task or to be reunited with their loved ones had, in even circumstances, the greatest chance to survive. It is an example of what I call the self-transcendent quality of a human being. Basically, a human being is never primarily concerned with himself or herself, or anything within himself or herself; but rather is reaching out into the world, out of himself or herself, into the world, toward a meaning to fulfill or another human being to love."

What kept Henri going was the thought that his Mother and twin sister, Margot, might still be alive. That possibility alone was enough to keep him struggling to survive.

"I always believed Margot was alive," Henri says. "Always. I think I would have known if she had not survived. It kept me going. As long as there was a chance that she was alive, I wanted to stay alive too, to help her, to be her family. We depended on each other."

As he recovered his strength, Henri focused on the need to find his sister and any other member of his family who might still be alive. Someone told him there was a Missing Persons Center in Krakow, a place where survivors, the homeless, and those who no longer had a country, could come for information on their loved ones.

It was hard to leave the comfort and security of his benefactors' home. They had treated him with great kindness. They had saved his legs and perhaps his life, asking nothing in return. They helped him simply because he was a human being who needed help. Though he cannot not remember their names Henri says he has never forgotten the lesson they taught him.

But in his heart he felt his sister was still alive. Although he was not so confident his mother still lived, he was hopeful. He had to find them if he could.

Henri made his way from Czechoslovakia to Krakow, traveling mostly on foot. There he found work in a dentist's office, sleeping on the couch in the office, while he continued his search. Each day around one o'clock, he took the trolley to the Missing Persons Center to see if there was any news about Margot or his other relatives. It was a sad place filled with people hoping for a happy ending. Not many were so fortunate.

One day on the trolley car, he saw a woman who looked familiar. He wasn't sure who she was, but something about her face, the line of her neck and her eyes, reminded him of someone he felt he knew. When the trolley stopped and she got off, Henri followed her. He trailed her for a block trying to confirm his impression and figure out what to say to her. Finally, he called out and asked her to please stop.

The woman stopped and turned. When she saw the intense, skinny man behind her, she drew back in fright. She told Henri to leave her alone or she would call the police.

Without knowing why, Henri shouted his mother's name – Fanny Landwirth! – as she walked away.

The woman stopped dead in her tracks. "How do you know that name?" she asked.

"She is my mother," Henri said.

"Oh God!" the woman exclaimed. "I am Mrs. Zawuska. Your mother was my best friend before the Germans came to Poland."

They talked on the street for a long time. Henri told her his story. He told her where he had been, where he now worked, and why he was there. When they parted, he left with renewed hope.

The next day, a chauffeured limousine arrived at the dentist's office. The driver said he had orders to pick up Henri and bring his things. He told Henri he would now be living with Mr. and Mrs. Zawuska.

Henri had known Mrs. Zawuska was well off from the way she dressed, but he had no idea she was wealthy. Nor did he have any idea she would want to take him in, but he was still sick and weak and trying to recover his sense of self. He went willingly.

The Zawuskas tended to Henri's condition, bringing the best doctors they could find in to see him. When the doctors concluded Henri had suffered a nervous breakdown, the couple gave up their home for more than a month so that Henri could have the peace and quiet the doctors said he needed.

There he received the news of his mother's death. He was heartbroken to learn she had died in one of the last acts of hate of a hate filled war. But three weeks later, he heard something more positive. A woman he met at the Missing Persons Center said Margot was still alive and living in a small town in the center of Germany.

The town was 500 miles from Krakow. Though the Zawuskas counseled against it, arguing he was not well enough to travel so far alone, Henri set out the next day. He took a backpack and traveled by foot, hitching a ride whenever he could. It took him six weeks to reach the city where someone said Margot had been seen.

"The whole time I was walking to this place, I was focused only on getting there," Henri recalls. "Now, as I walked into this town, my heart started pounding in my chest. I had come all this way and now stood in the place I set out to find, but I was afraid I would be disappointed."

For a while, Henri just stood there, frozen by uncertainty and the fear of being disappointed. Then, as the beating of his heart calmed, he began asking everyone he saw if they knew Margot. He went from house to house, up one street and down another. He asked every stranger he saw if they had seen Margot.

Just as he was about to give up, one of the townsmen told him there were a few survivors living on the other side of town. If Margot lived, he said, they might know where to find her.

Henri ran to the place described. He found the house where the survivors were said to live and quickly approached a man working in the yard.

"Do you know Margot Landwirth?" Henri asked.

The man shook his head. His gesture had the impact of a punch to the stomach.

"Are you sure?"

"There is no one by that name here."

"Is this the place where the survivors live?" Henri persisted.

The man said it was.

When they were children, Margot and Henri had a secret whistle, a whistle only they knew. It was their way to call each other. As Henri stood there that distant memory came back to him. He caught his breath and started to whistle as loudly as he could.

Within moments he heard Margot's response. He had found her.

"I did not know there was such joy left in the world," Henri says. "Finding Margot amid the ruins, finding love and hope, hearing her whistle, knowing after all these years she survived—What a gift! It was a miracle."

CHAPTER NINE

"Each of us has within us a Mother Teresa and a Hitler.

It is up to us to chose what we want to be."

...ELIZABETH KUBLER-ROSS

"No one has the right to do wrong," Frankl said, "not even if wrong has been done to them. I can still see the prisoner who rolled up his shirt sleeves, thrust his right hand under my nose and shouted, 'May this hand be cut off if I don't stain it with blood on the day I get home!' I want to emphasize that the man who said these words was not a bad fellow. He had been the best of comrades in the camps and afterwards."

Hate breeds hate. Hurt and humiliation seek vengeance and retribution. After the war, thousand of Jews wanted to get even. Henri was among their number.

Five years of starvation, humiliation, degradation and death had left him consumed by hate. He felt compelled to take some action, any action against those who had caused so much pain to people he loved and so many other innocent human beings.

"I was filled with a child's need to hurt others as I had been hurt," Henri says, "thinking this would help fill the empty places in my life and replace what had been lost."

Margot fell in love and married but for Henri during the dark year of 1946, it seemed the need to express his hate was all there was. He was a nineteen-year old boy looking for revenge.

The Allies were rounding up Nazi soldiers, collaborators and sympathizers. Jews who had survived the camp were treated with sympathy and given a lot of latitude.

On the eastern front, Jews were put in positions of power. Stalin made a Jew whose father had died in Treblinka chief of the Office of State Security. Jews were placed in charge of intelligence, imprisonment, and appointed security chiefs for occupied territories.

Many Jews found this only fitting and appropriate. They assumed, as one writer has noted, the Allies wanted the Nazis pursued by the hounds of hell: themselves.

And pursue they did.

On October 17, 1945, for example, Poland decreed every German who wasn't in jail must leave Poland and Poland-administered Germany. Polish police rounded up and herded on to trains some ten million people. It was the largest forced migration in human history. Over the next three years, it is estimated sixty to eighty thousand Germans in camps and prisons were killed in reprisal for the holocaust.

"We wanted the Germans to suffer as they had made us suffer," Henri says.

Since he spoke German, Polish, and Russian, Henri was valuable to the Russians and the Americans trying to identify former Nazis. One of the jobs he was given was the task of evicting Nazis and Nazi sympathizers so that American and Russian families could occupy their houses.

"In nine out of ten cases, when we walked in one German would fall all over himself giving us the name of another German," Henri recalls. "He would say, 'Maybe I was a Nazi, but the guy down the street was a real Nazi. I was a little guy, he was a leader, a big Nazi.' They made my work very easy to do."

"I had no sympathy for them whatsoever. I felt nothing but hatred for the Germans. If a German didn't leave, I threw him out onto the street. I told him his house wasn't his anymore – and I meant it. When they begged me for mercy, I didn't hear them. I thought of my mother and father and I didn't hear them at all."

In addition, Henri became part of a gang, a band of survivors that began smuggling commodities in short supply across the borders into Poland and worked with the Jewish Underground.

"We did crazy things," he says. "To us there was no law. Nothing mattered."

Sometimes an entire life can turn on a single moment. Instead of dissipating, the hatred Henri felt had only grown as he expressed it. He found every opportunity to pick a fight with former Nazis. He beat them up because of who they were and what he felt they had done or allowed to be done.

Walking along a river between two towns one fateful day, Henri came upon a German boy. He was about the same age as Henri had been when he was taken. The boy was dressed in the uniform of the Hitler Jurgen, Hitler's youth organization.

"He wore the black leather pants and shirt. He was proud of himself. I could tell that," Henri recalls.

Henri blocked the boy's way and asked if he was a good Hitler Jurgen. He could see the fear in his eyes. It was just the two of them.

"I wanted to hurt him in some way. I wanted to do to him what they had done me. I told him to strip naked or I was going to kill him – those were my very words: Take off your clothes or I'm going to kill you!"

Realizing Henri was serious, the boy quickly started to undress. He took off everything but his underwear.

Henri told him to take them off, too. "I was so angry, I think if he had refused, I would have actually killed him with my bare hands."

The boy did as he was told. Henri picked up his clothes and threw them in the river. He hated this boy and everything his uniform stood for.

The boy stood naked before his tormentor, as Henri had done so many times before, shivering and afraid in the face of unreasoning hate. As Henri looked at the boy, the rage he had been carrying crested. Five years of humiliation and torture, made his blood boil.

"Maybe I'll just kill him," Henri thought and grabbed the boy by the neck. "I'll strangle him with my bare hands."

Then from deep inside came a quiet thought. He did not want to be like them.

"I did not want to become what I despised," Henri says. "Anything would be better than turning into one of them."

Slowly, the rage subsided. When he caught his breath, he released the boy and told him to run. It would be many years before he could say he forgave the Germans, but he had turned compassion's corner. The healing had begun.

CHAPTER TEN

"America is another name for opportunity."

...RALPH WALDO EMERSON

Americans of German descent are the largest ethnic group in the United States. Understandably, immigration from Germany to the United States slowed to a trickle during World War II. The U. S. Census reports there are around 45 million German-Americans in the United States. Less than 10,000 were admitted in 1945. Most of these were German Jews.

In June of 1945, Secretary of State Cordell Hull personally approved the admission of Wernher von Braun and his closest associates to the United States. Since the paperwork of those selected for admission to the United States was marked by paperclips, von Braun and his colleagues became part of a project that has come to be known as Operation Paperclip, a program that resulted in the employment of German scientist formerly considered war criminals or security threats by the U. S. Army.

Von Braun and his staff were transferred to Fort Bliss, Texas. Their first assignment was to train American personnel in the intricacies of rockets and guided missiles. Under their guidance, the first reassembled V-2 rocket was successfully launched at the White Sands Proving Grounds in New Mexico on June 28, 1946.

Henri arrived in the United States by freighter, much like the one that had carried the Nazi's V-2 rockets and their spare parts to America at the end of the war.

He had returned to Belgium in 1947 and went to work for his Uncle Herman, a diamond broker. Uncle Herman put Henri to work in his factory and taught him the art of cutting stones. But it wasn't long before Henri began feeling restless. He longed for a new life in a new land. America called him.

"I wanted to go to America to see if the stories I had heard were true," he said, "a land where anything is possible, a place where I could start over and become anything I dared to dream."

With only his dreams and desire, Henri went down to the dock in Antwerp hoping to find a boat going to America that needed a crewmember willing to work for passage. He made the trip every day for several weeks until one of the dock-workers pointed out a ship that needed crewmembers.

Henri left Belgium with the clothes on his back. The only thing in his pockets was a $20 bill his cousin, Kitty Birnbaum, had given him for the journey. After five weeks cleaning latrines and working as a deck laborer, his ship sailed into New York Harbor.

"It is difficult to express my feelings as I arrived in America," Henri says. "I felt so many emotions at once – joy, fear, happiness, melancholy. I missed my parents, my sister and the rest of my family. But at the same time, I was excited to see America. I had dreamed about it for so long. As I looked at the Statue of Liberty, I did not think of all the bad things that happened to me, only the possibilities opening up before me."

America is the land of opportunity, but no one ever promised it would be easy. Dreams of a good job and an easy life quickly vanished in the hard reality of New York. Though Henri was fluent in several languages, he did not speak English. He had a sponsor, his Aunt Selma and Uncle Ernest, and a place to live, their apartment in Jackson Heights, but he needed a job.

In Belgium, he had become adept at cutting stones so the day after he arrived in New York Henri headed for the diamond district. He found work immediately only to discover the differences between Europe and the New World carried over to the way they cut stones. He had to retrain himself to cut diamonds the way they were cut in America.

"In Antwerp, cutting diamonds was an art. In the United States, it was all production, numbers, and gross quantity. I had to stop being an artist or I wouldn't earn enough money to live."

Henri learned to adapt, but he wasn't happy about it. The size of the city, the crowd and dirt, began to wear on him. He was homesick. He missed his sister and the rest of his family and decided to go back to Belgium to attend his cousin Kitty's wedding.

As soon as he boarded the ship returning to Europe, Henri realized he no more wanted to return to Europe than he wanted to stay in New York. What he wanted was a place in America more suitable to his needs. When he returned, he knew things would be better. He would find a way to make a success of his life no matter how hard it was to get started.

Sure enough, things began to improve almost immediately on his return. He began to feel more confident of himself and more comfortable in America. Then in January 1950, he received a telegram.

"At first I thought it was a joke," Henri remembers. "Who is this sending me telegrams and signing the name of the President of the United States?"

But it was no joke. Henri, now 23 years old, had been drafted.

Henri was ordered to report to Fort Devens, Massachusetts. A few months later, he was sent to Fort Dix and on his way to Korea when an officer noticed he had been a diamond cutter. At the time, the U.S. Army relied on crystals for tuning sensitivity in their field radios. There was a shortage of people experienced in working with these crystals. The officer reasoned if Henri could cut diamonds, he could cut crystals, too. He was pulled from the infantry and given amended orders making him a stateside crystal cutter. He was assigned to the radio shack for the First Army at Fort Dix.

At first it seemed like an inconvenience and an interruption, but Henri now sees the two years he spent in the Army as the best thing that could have happened to him. Serving in the Army helped him get a better feel for life in America. When he was discharged, he had more self-confidence and even more determination to take advantage of the opportunity America provided.

"Opportunities unavailable anywhere else on earth are open to every person here, regardless of where a person was born, their race or social class," Henri says. "There were no closed borders with guards who could demand to see my papers and detain me on a whim. There was only opportunity, real opportunity, opportunity that allowed anyone who was willing to start at the bottom and work hard to make a success of their life."

Unlike most Americans, Henri has a measure by which to compare the joys available in this country.

"If every American had the same experience I did," he says, "no one would ever take what we have in America for granted. Where else but America could a person like me have an opportunity to meet heads of state, to become lifetime friends and business partners with America's first astronauts, and fulfill all his dreams?"

CHAPTER ELEVEN

"The reason a lot of people do not recognize opportunity

is because it usually goes around wearing

overalls looking like work."

...THOMAS EDISON

The year Henri was released from the Army, Von Braun and his team were transferred from Texas to Huntsville, Alabama. Shortly after he arrived, the Huntsville Times ran a front-page story, with the headline: "Dr. von Braun Says Rocket Flights Possible to Moon."

Von Braun thought American's devotion to space fiction could be channeled into interest in space fact. According to his biographer, Erik Bergaust, von Braun believed it was simply "a matter of synthesizing the philosophical aspects into neat packages and solid statements the public would buy."

In early 1950, Von Braun began laying out his vision for the American public in Collier's magazine. Next, he turned to television. Collier's had a circulation of 4 million, but nowhere near the influence of television, which was coming into its own. Von Braun quickly realized this medium had the potential to fundamentally reshape American's perceptions. He found an ally in Walt Disney, who shared his view of the power of television. During the next few years von Braun would serve as technical advisor on three Disney productions exploring the possibility of space travel.

While von Braun did his best to build public interest and keep his dream alive, his life-long desire to explore space remained subordinated to military needs. For most of the decade, he led the Army's rocket team at Redstone Arsenal, developing the Redstone rocket.

⚫

Meanwhile, Henri was at a crossroad. His service in the military had given him time to think and a new perspective on the world. He had no control of his life when he was young. Now he was in a new land with no restrains beyond his interests and ability. What did he want to do with his life? How and where did he want to live?

The hospitality industry innately appealed to him. It was accessible. He would not need a college education. There were plenty of entry-level positions available. It was a people-centered industry with the potential for on-the job training. With these thoughts in mind, he decided to give it try, taking whatever jobs he could find in the hotel business. At one point or another, he did every thing there was to do in a hotel, from changing linen and cleaning bathrooms to managing the front desk.

"I tried to do everything with tremendous passion," Henri says, "whatever it was. I wanted to prove I could succeed in this great country. It did not matter what the job was, I tried to do it as if it was the most important job in the world. I tried to be the best bellhop, or the best floor sweeper—every job I took, I tried to do the best job I could."

In November of 1952, Henri took a job at the night desk of the Wellington Hotel in New York. About the same time, he used his GI Bill benefits to enroll in the New York Hotel Technology School. Between the two, he quickly learned the fundamentals of hotel management.

"Most businesses are based on pleasing people," Henri says. "If you want to be successful in business, first you have to be successful with people. If you want to be successful with people, you have to give them what they want. You have to understand what customers need. The best way to learn that is not to talk, but listen. If you really listen, the customer will always tell you what they want."

Two years later, Henri and his first wife, Josephine Guarino, visited Miami Beach on their honeymoon. It was warm and a long way from New York. Both of these things appealed to Henri a great deal. He decided to stay.

With that decision, Henri went looking for a job in Miami

Beach. When he couldn't immediately find one in the hotel business, he took a job in Burdines Department Store. A month later he got a call from the manager of the President Madison Hotel, one of the hotels he had applied to earlier. The manager said he had a job that paid $75 a week. Since Henri did not have "Miami Beach" experience, he was told he would have to settle for $65.

Some would have walked away but for Henri it offered the opportunity to do what he wanted to do in a place he wanted be. He took the job and soon had more than enough "Miami Beach" experience.

Conditions at the President Madison were terrible. The night manager was an alcoholic, more interested in drinking than working. He was more than happy to let Henri do his job. Henri was more than happy to do it. When others took similar advantage, Henri viewed it as a learning opportunity.

"Any time somebody didn't want to work, they would call me," Henri remembers. "I was the broom of that outfit. On New Years and Christmas, when nobody wanted to work, I worked. When the housekeeper went on vacation, I did her job. I pushed the maid's cart and cleaned rooms and bathrooms. Whatever they wanted, I did without complaint."

In the process, Henri got the education he needed. He also earned the owner's trust.

A year later, Henri was working at the Fountain Bleu Hotel

when his old boss from the President Madison, Sidney Raffle, called. Raffle said he wanted Henri back as his night clerk. The only problem was Henri was now making twice as much at the Fountain Bleu.

Raffle talked with his partners and agreed to give Henri what he was making at the Fountain Bleu—$120 a week. They sweetened the deal by giving him the title of assistant manager. He came back in charge of all the people that had taken advantage of him before.

Three months later when the manager of the Hotel was fired, Henri assumed his responsibilities as temporary manager. The next day he fired two of the hotel's long-term employees. Raffle was furious until Henri explained they were taking advantage of him by not booking rooms they rented so they could pocket the money themselves. With that, Henri was given full rein of the hotel.

Under Henri's management, the hotel prospered. "My answer to a hotel's problems was always to try and find the solution that was best for the customer," he says.

In 1954, a small solution provided a big dividend. A guest at the Hotel asked where he could by a tie so that he could eat in the Hotel's dining room. The dining room required men to wear a necktie and he didn't have one.

Without hesitation, Henri said, "Here, you can borrow this one." He took off his own tie—the only tie he owned—and gave it to a stranger.

After dinner the man came back. He returned the tie and introduced himself. He said his name was B.G. McNabb. The two talked for a few minutes before McNabb left.

Henri would later learn the man he had befriended was General Manager of the Intercontinental Ballistic Missile Division of General Dynamics. He was one of the pioneers of the space program, charged with bringing Cape Canaveral to life.

When McNabb went to the Cape in 1955, he realized his most significant problem was the lack of housing in Cocoa Beach. He needed to create homes for employees coming in from all over the country and a lodging where transient workers could stay. He had to build it all, including a motel to house the people who would construct the site.

All the big hotel chains had turned him down. They could only see what Cocoa Beach was. They could not imagine what Cape Canaveral would become. The motel would be called The Starlight Motel, McNabb said. Men who would reach for the stars would live there, but they could not see it.

Someone had told McNabb to talk to Sid Raffle. Raffle was known to be the kind of guy who trusted his instincts and had a reputation for getting things done. When McNabb explained the Air Force would guarantee 30 rooms a day 365 days a year if Raffle would build the hotel and that Boeing, North American Rockwell, Lockheed and other contractors were

ame kind of guarantees, Raffle readily

otel was almost finished, Raffle intro-
n he had picked to manage the new
nstant dislike to him and told Raffle
l, he remembered a skinny guy he
dison Hotel.

" McNabb said, "but he had a

fu   "

March 7, 2006, Founder's Day at Give Kids the World, Henri Landwirth's 79th birthday and Give Kids the World's twentieth anniversary. Henri is pictured here with two of the 83,000 children Give Kids the World has served.

Max Landwirth, Henri's father, was arrested in 1939 and taken to a prison called Radom. No charges were filed against him but one morning without ceremony or notice, he was marched to the killing fields along with a number of other prisoners, shot, and buried in an unmarked grave.

Fanny Landwirth, Henri's mother, survived until near the end of the war when she was herded on to a ship with 2,000 other women. The ship was taken out into the harbor and blown-up.

Henri and Margot were born five minutes apart. The twins were separated at the age of 13 when Henri was sent to the Plaszow work camp. They were reunited after the war.

Henri outside the apartment in Krakow where his family was forced to live. "They came to our house," Henri remembers, "and gave us a few hours to get ready. We were herded like animals into the poorest sections of Krakow where they built a ten-foot wall around us."

Henri at the switching yard in Auschwitz. "This is where my destiny was de-cided," he said, "I remember it like it was yesterday."

In 1973, Henri returned to Mauthausen with his sons Gary and Greg. The average survival period for prisoners at Mauthausen was four months. Henri would last for more than nine months there before being sent somewhere worse.

In Belgium after the War, Henri had become adept at cutting stones. He arrived in America in 1948 with $20 in his pocket and immediately sought work in New York's diamond district.

In January 1950, Henri received a telegram from the President of the United States. At first he thought it was a joke. To his surprise, he learned he was drafted for Korea. He is pictured here with his basic training unit.

The Starlite Hotel was the first hotel on Cocoa Beach. It would become home to men who would reach for the stars.

Henri with Walter Cronkite in Cocoa Beach. Cronkite's broadcast of his news program from the front of Henri's hotel helped put Holiday Inns on the map.

Henri became lifelong friends with The Mercury 7 Astronauts. He is pictured here in 1990 with Deke Slayton, Walter Cronkite, Gordon Cooper, and John Glenn.

When Disney announced it was coming to Orlando, Henri and John Glenn immediately went to Memphis to talk with Holiday Inns about acquiring a franchise for that territory. They returned with not one, but several franchises, forging a partnership in the process with John Quinn. This partnership would last for more than forty years.

Theme park characters from all the parks visit Give Kids the World Village on a regular basis. Disney characters join Henri here in welcoming children to the Castle of Miracles.

Henri with wish children and Mayor Clayton at the Amberville Train Station.

Henri knew his vision for Give Kids the World would only work if Disney was involved. When Disney approved, he quickly set up a meeting with Sea World and Universal. He is pictured here with Dick Nunis, Past President of Disney World, and Bob Gault, Past President of Universal Studios, celebrating twenty years of making dreams come true.

In 2001, shortly after this photograph with his wife, Linda, was taken, Henri returned to Poland with a film crew preparing a documentary on his life. Two days after shooting wrapped up, he had a stroke. Fortunately, Linda recognized the symptoms and called an ambulance. He was able to make a full recovery.

The Landwirth family, proof of the failure of Hitler's grand design, at Henri's 80th birthday reunion. April 2007. Front row (from left): Grandchildren:Sarah Ussery, Emily Ussery, Rebecca Landwirth, Max Landwirth. Back row (from left): Lisa Ussery, Linda and Henri Landwirth, Jillian Alpert, Greg Landwirth, Theresa and Gary Landwirth.

CHAPTER TWELVE

"The highest reward for a person's toil is not what

they get for it, but what they become by it."

...JOHN RUSKIN

When Henri arrived at Cocoa Beach, there were lots of palmetto bugs and mosquitoes, one restaurant and two gas stations in the town. There were 823 registered voters.

Wayne Headley, the town marshal, used his own car for police business. He also ran Cocoa Beach's Volunteer Fire Department. There were no traffic lights and more cars on the beach than on the road.

It was 1957, seven years after Henri got off the freighter that had brought him to the New World and five years after he decided to try the hotel business. He was 28 years old, about the same age as the men who would ride America's first rockets into space.

The Starlight Motel was nearing completion. Sid Raffle had guided that project while McNabb built 139 homes in twelve months for the people who would have permanent positions at the Cape. McNabb was a man of action, used to making things happen.

In 1945, McNabb had launched America's first guided missiles from the Naval Weapons Test Center in California. He then served as director of research on the hydrogen bomb project before General Dynamics hired him to build America's launching center.

A short man with deeply tanned skin and a quick fuse, McNabb was strict and demanding. He left no doubt he was a man on a mission with little time to spare. Later, he described those early days at the Cape.

"There was a feeling in the air that what we were doing was important to the future of America," he said. "The people who came to work at the Cape all shared in this sense of mission. It was an incredibly focused time. Men worked their asses off in the day and partied their asses off at night. That is just the way it was. There wasn't so much of a class thing as there is today. The NASA boys and the building contractors and the flyboys, everybody was together. We worked together and we played together. And together, we built the Cape."

From the day The Starlight Motel opened, it was a huge success. Room occupancy was at capacity year round. "Without exaggeration," Henri says, "the money was just coming in through the windows. We couldn't do anything wrong. It was a great hotel."

There were 99 rooms, a bakery, coffee shop, and dining room, but what made the Motel the legend it became was its bar, The Starlight Lounge. The Starlight Lounge became the social center for people who lived and worked at the Cape.

In keeping with it's setting, Henri had high quality black lights installed in the Lounge. He brought in artists and asked them to paint scenes from space that would pop out of the walls when the lights were turned on. He hired top talent to provide entertainment and staffed the Starlight with the best-looking, most personable women he could find.

"I loved the Starlight Lounge," Mercury 7 Astronaut Gordo Cooper remembers. "When you turned those black lights on, you could see these lunar scenes with landing vehicles sitting near big craters. The place would kind of glow. I thought it was neat and fit the clientele—pilots and dreamers who were working their butts off to get into space."

"The magical thing about The Starlight was the diversity of people that came together there," Henri says. "From the chairman and presidents of America's biggest companies to the guys laying cable and digging ditches, The Starlight brought them all together."

One of those was Werhner von Braun. He had no way of knowing his host was once his guest in the mountains at Mittlebau.

In 1955, Disney released a series called "Man in the Moon." The film presented a "realistic and believable trip to the moon in a rocket ship." Von Braun, complete with a slide rule in his pocket, narrated portions of the film and described his vision of a voyage to the moon. Forty-two million people saw the series.

Largely in response to the growing interest in space, on July 29, 1955 President Eisenhower announced the United States would launch an unmanned, earth-circling satellite within two years. Meanwhile, the Soviets were feverishly working on their own rocket designs and the Sputnik program. With the launch of Sputnik in 1957, the race for space began.

The National Aeronautics and Space Administration, NASA, was established by law on July 29, 1958. When NASA opened the Marshall Space Flight Center in Huntsville, Alabama, Wernher von Braun was named the Center's first Director. The Marshall Center's first major program was development of the Saturn rockets to carry heavy payloads into and beyond Earth's orbit.

The pressure of the space race was enormous. The Starlight Lounge became the place where those feeling the pressure went to let off steam and the place to go to when a celebration was in order.

"We celebrated every success," Henri recalls. "I was awed by what these men were accomplishing. I felt it was an honor to celebrate with them when things went well and to help boost their morale when things weren't so good."

In 1959, an ICBM with a Christmas message from President Eisenhower was launched into space. As it orbited around the world, the unmanned rocket transmitted the President's holiday greeting of peace on earth and good will to all.

Henri thought this was a very American effort and was thrilled to be part of it. To help celebrate McNabb's accomplishment, he sent a driver to the Cape to pick him up.

When McNabb arrived at the Starlight, Henri said, "I don't know how to thank you on behalf of America but I do know you have always been a frustrated hotel manger."

He handed McNabb the keys. "Here you go," he said. "You are the manager of this hotel. You can do anything you want. Go for it."

McNabb had his assistants get on the phone and call all the technicians and engineers involved in the project and invited them to celebrate at The Starlight. Hundreds of people showed up for free food and drinks. Word spread and even more people arrived. The party got bigger and bigger until the Lounge was crammed to capacity.

Finally, Henri said, "B.G., I hope you are having fun, because it looks like I'm going broke now!"

Two years after it opened, The Starlight Motel was sold. Sid Raffle informed Henri by letter.

"It was really a shame," Henri said, "but I couldn't blame him. Hotels and motels are sold by occupancy. With nearly a hundred percent occupancy year round, selling it was good business. Raffle made a lot of money."

CHAPTER THIRTEEN

"There never was a person who did anything

worth doing that did not receive

more than he gave."

...HENRY WARD BECHER

Henri didn't know what to do. He had not profited from the sale of the hotel he helped make so successful. He had little money and nowhere to go. The Starlight Motel was still the only game in town.

Wanting to stay in the area, he decided to lease a 14-room hotel on the river between Cocoa Beach and Titusville. He called it the Space Motel with the hope the Cape would expand in his direction and make his tiny new motel successful.

Henri moved his wife and two sons into a small apartment behind the motel and began remodeling. Within a few months, business began to pick up. Before long, the Space Motel became to Titusville what The Starlight Lounge was to Cocoa

Beach. Saturday nights in the bar were standing room only.

Henri was starting to have fun again when ABC agents closed him down. The Space Motel had a restricted alcohol license. Liquor could only be served as long as food was available. He was accused of violating this law and slapped with a $500 fine.

While he fought the charges that had been brought against him, he received an offer from Holiday Inn. They wanted him to oversee the building of a new hotel in Cocoa Beach and manage it when it opened. His initial thought was to turn it down and stay on his own. After discussing it with his wife, he reconsidered and accepted Holiday Inn's proposal.

Later, Henri would find out he was again indebted to B.G. McNabb.

Knowing of his influence in Cocoa Beach, Holiday Inns had approached McNabb for advice. McNabb met with a representative of Holiday Inns in his home, talking the proposal over at length. The two men got so far as to actually design the lay out of the hotel on a scratchpad when the Holiday Inn representative asked McNabb if he would be willing to give the new hotel some of his business.

"McNabb told them the only way he would ever consider it is if they would hire me as a manager," Henri says.

From collectSPACE, a blog for space junkies:

Dave: Which hotel in Cocoa Beach do you believe represented the hub of the action during the 60's space race?

KC Stoever (Scott Carpenter's daughter): That's easy. The Holiday Inn, managed by the legendary Henri Landwirth.

Henri returned to Cocoa Beach and began overseeing major construction of a hotel for the first time. While the hotel was being built, he called his friends from The Starlight days and let them know he was back in town. Like The Starlight, the Holiday Inn was a success from the moment it opened.

The bar at the Holiday Inn was called the Riviera Lounge. When the astronauts followed Henri to the Holiday Inn, it became the place to be in Cocoa Beach. It was also the place to play.

"During the early days at the Cape, we began a non-stop competition of practical jokes," Admiral Alan Shepard recalls. "I don't know how the practical jokes got started. Probably because, as a group, the astronauts were very intense, very focused, and very competitive. When you are working in an environment like that, there is always a need for comic relief. As for Henri, he just loved to pull pranks. He was always thinking of the next gag."

One morning Henri heard John Glenn complaining there weren't any towels in his room. As Glenn remembers it, he went down to the front desk acting very serious. "I banged on the desk and made a big fuss. There were a lot people checking in, but I just kept banging on the desk and asking, 'What do I have to do to get some towels around this place.' Finally, Henri came down. I gave him the business for a few minutes and then laughed, telling him I as only kidding."

The next time Glenn checked in he found a truckload of towels in his room.

"The tub was filled with towels," Glenn recalls. "The vanity was filled with towels. You couldn't see the bed. It was covered with towels piled up the ceiling. You could hardly close the door there were so many towels in that room."

Shepard caught a small alligator on a hunting trip. The next morning, he took the four-foot gator to Henri's pool and threw it in.

Upping the ante, McNabb bought a 19-foot cabin cruiser and launched it in the pool. He invited the press and had a cocktail party on his boat in Henri's pool at the Holiday Inn.

"All I could do was have a drink," Henri says, "and hope the boat didn't sink."

A few weeks later, Henri found Gordo Cooper sitting on the edge of the pool with a fishing pole. "What are you doing?" Henri asked.

"I'm fishing."

"But this is a swimming pool."

"I came here to fish and I am fishing," Cooper responded.

"It's swimming pool," Henri insisted. "There are no fish."

"There are now," Gordo said and dropped a cooler full of live fish into the swimming pool.

In 1962 when John Glenn's orbital flight was scheduled, Henri had his chef construct a 900 lb cake model of his capsule to celebrate. The cake was so large it had to be assembled in sections on a truck. As Glenn's flight was delayed, the cake had to be moved to a refrigerated truck. That made Henri wonder how they would get the cake off the truck in one piece when Glenn landed. At his request, McDonnell Aircraft agreed to build a special lift for the occasion.

All this was supposed to be a secret, but as he started re-entry on Friendship 7, Glenn was heard to say over his radio, "Henri, I'm coming home. Get the cake ready."

One morning, Henri stopped by Walter Cronkite's room to visit and see if he was comfortable. Cronkite was talking with his producer, Don Hewitt. They thanked Henri for his hospitality and asked if there was anything *they* could do for *him*.

Henri couldn't think of anything.

"How about this," Hewitt said. "Walter, what if we do your Sunday Evening News segment outside in front of the Holiday Inn sign?"

Cronkite liked the idea. At the time, his weekly broadcast was the highest rated television show in the country. Holiday Inn was just beginning to grow with 200 hotels in operation. After the 15 minutes of solid airtime Cronkite's favor provided, that number quickly grew. Later that year, Holiday Inns gave Henri their lifetime achievement award for helping to put the franchise on the map.

CHAPTER FOURTEEN

"What is the essence of life?

To serve others and do good."

...ARISTOTLE

The Holiday Inn at Cocoa Beach was so successful the President of Holiday Inns, Kemmons Wilson, promised Henri a franchise whenever he was financially ready. All Henri had to do was pick a spot, Wilson said, and he could have it.

In 1966, when Disney announced it was of coming to Orlando, Henri immediately saw the opportunity. He called John Glenn and suggested they go into business there together.

"When I looked at central Florida on a map, I could see the most likely place for anything to happen was where Highway I-4 and Highway 27 came together," Henri said. "So that was the place we decided to build our hotel."

With their location in mind, Glenn and Henri went to Memphis to talk with Holiday Inns. They returned with not one, but several franchises. Fortuitously, on the plane back

Henri met John Quinn. Quinn had been in Memphis for the same reason, returning with the rights to a franchise in North Orlando's Altamonte Springs.

Quinn had a background in commercial real estate and financial planning. The two men hit it off and agreed to form a three-way partnership. As part of the arrangement, Henri assumed responsibility for building both hotels and managing the properties.

"As soon as we broke ground I called my partners and told them we had to expand Disney East by 72 rooms," Henri said.

He had picked his location well. The property was located 3 miles from what would soon be Disney's front gate. From the day it opened, the property was at near capacity.

At Disney East, Henri catered to families, creating the kid-sensitive environment that would become his trademark. Altamonte Springs catered to business travelers. It was a commercial property having problems distinguishing itself and attracting customers in a crowded market.

Henri focused on the surrounding area and found there were a lot of students and people who worked for Disney, living in apartments nearby.

"The young people needed a place where they could meet, have a beer, and spend some time together," Henri says. His answer was The Why Not Lounge.

Anyone familiar with Orlando in the sixties will remember

The Why Not Lounge. Henri set aside a special area where young people could socialize and charged them a dime for an omelet. Next, he added Cuban sandwiches for a dime an inch. Henri hired two bands so there could be continuous music. When one stopped playing, the other began. Then, he started a club for women, offering members drinks for nickel. That attracted the girls, which in turn brought in the guys.

As the bar's reputation grew, it was expanded into the dining room. Before he was done, Henri would move the location of the band four times. Each time he moved it, he added a new dance floor. The Why Not Lounge became the only club in the area offering multiple dance floors.

When the bar became so notorious it was written up in Playboy Magazine, Henri knew it was time to sell. The partners sold the establishment at the height of its popularity.

As he became successful, increasingly Henri felt the need to give back. He started a family foundation, naming it after his mother, and encouraged the original astronauts to do something that would bind them together forever. The result was the Mercury 7 Foundation, established to provide scholarships for promising students.

When the Gemini astronauts were added to the program, Henri conspired with Pete Conrad to bring the two groups together. Up until then, the Mercury 7 astronauts were tightly knit, keeping mostly to themselves. The Gemini astronauts were too intimidated to infringe on the group. Henri and Conrad, one of the astronauts who would eventually go to the moon, felt it was important to get all the astronauts together. They planned an elaborate social event for that purpose.

Without Conrad's knowledge, Henri added his own touch. He told his chef to prepare a dinner for the astronauts they would never forget.

"We had fancy menus that said the main course was veal cutlets and baked potatoes," Shepard recalled. "We had white table clothes and fine china. There were waitresses all over the place, serving wine in these lovely crystal glasses. It was really elegant. No one had any idea what Henri was up to."

After the astronauts had a chance to get to know each other, the main course was served.

"Nobody could even get a knife into it," Cooper remembers. "Henri had the cook take thick pieces of cardboard, bread them and deep fry them so they looked like veal. On top of that, the potatoes were raw, but there was cheese melted on top so you couldn't tell."

Shepard tried to cut into the cardboard and decided he could do without the veal. "I couldn't get my knife to go through it," he said. "I tried the vegetable – broccoli I think – and it was raw. I didn't even bother with the potato."

"I sat next to Gordo and watched him," Henri says. "I didn't want

him to put that cardboard thing in his mouth and have to have his stomach pumped. His flight was scheduled for the next morning."

After a few minutes, the astronauts caught on and threw their cardboard steaks at Henri. The ice had been broken. The spirit forged that evening carried over. In 1987, the Mercury 7 Foundation was expanded to include other astronauts and renamed the Astronaut Scholarship Foundation. To date, more than 70 astronauts from the Mercury, Gemini, Apollo, Skylab, and Shuttle programs have become involved, awarding $2.3 million in scholarships to deserving students.

At all of his hotels, Henri focused on family. "If you get passed the suits," he says, "the business traveler is a mother, father, grandparent, aunt or uncle, son or daughter. If you fulfill the needs of the people who stay in the hotel, they will fill your rooms."

In each hotel, this philosophy was reinforced and expanded. The "children's room" concept Henri developed when he began was refined by two of Henri's employees, Terry Whaples and Jim Olsen, with the creation of "kid's suites" at the Holiday Inn Sunspree. This family friendly concept worked so well it has been adopted by Holiday Inns and expanded to 20 Holiday Inn Kid's Suites worldwide.

In 2005, this concept was taken to another level with creation of the first Nickelodeon-themed hotel in the world. Howard Smith, Senior Vice President of Nickelodeon, proposed the idea. Steve Porter, President of Intercontinental Hotels Group, and Mark Snyder, Senior Vice President for Brand Management for Holiday Inns and Holiday Inns Express, hammered out the details.

"We originally looked into building our own hotel," Smith, explained, "but we found that the Holiday Inn Family Suites Resort had the ideal design and management team to communicate Nickelodeon's sensibility and our connection with kids."

The Holiday Inn Family Suites Resort had been voted the best Holiday Inn in North America by InterContinental Hotels Groups Priority Members in each of the three years preceding years. When it reopened as the Nickelodeon Family Suites by Holiday Inn, it was an immediate sensation; averaging 3 million hits on the internet each month.

Wernher von Braun's life-long dream to help mankind set foot on the moon became a reality on July 16, 1969 when a Marshall-developed Saturn V rocket launched the crew of Apollo 11 on its historic eight-day mission. With his mission accomplish, he retired in 1972.

Von Braun died of cancer in 1977. After his death *Life Magazine* called him the father of the United States space program and named him one of the "100 Most Important Americans of the 20th Century."

Two years later, the U. S. Congress opened a special investigation to uncover Nazi war criminals living in the United States. The investigation implicated Arthur Rudolph, von Braun's deputy, for the use of slave labor at V-2 production sites during the war.

In 1984 Rudolph renounced his citizenship and returned to Germany to avoid prosecution for possible war crimes. Rudolph had directed V-2 production at Dora-Mittelbau where Henri was interred before coming to the United States with other German Scientists. At NASA, Rudolph managed production of the Saturn 5 rocket and the Pershing missile under von Braun's direction.

CHAPTER FIFTEEN

"We make a living by what we get;

we make a life by what we give."

...WINSTON CHURCHILL

In 1986, one of the many wish granting groups in the United States called one of Henri's hotels and asked if he would help make a little girl's wish come true. Her name was Amy. She was six years old with incurable cancer. More than anything else, she said, she would like to meet Mickey Mouse.

It was a simple wish. The kind of thing wish granting groups are used to hearing. All they wanted from Henri was a room. Understandably, he did not have to be persuaded.

When he asked his manager about her a week later, Henri was shocked to hear the girl never arrived. She had died before all the arrangements could be made to bring her to Orlando.

"I hurt for the family's loss," Henri remembers, *"but I also felt angry. How could this happen? For days, I couldn't stop thinking about Amy and her family. What if another family simply ran out of time?"*

The thought bothered him enough that Henri started looking into the way wish foundations worked. Though he didn't know it, the death of this child had united his past with his present.

Henri learned nearly three fourths of all terminally ill children share Amy's desire. Most of them have never traveled outside their own communities. Their families, burdened by the battle to keep their child alive, have neither the time nor the resources to think about taking a vacation from death.

Arranging these trips was a complicated affair. Wish granting groups typically took six to eight weeks to process a child's request and make the necessary arrangements for travel, tickets, and hotels.

As Amy reminded him, sometimes six or eight weeks can make the difference between life and death. There has to be a better way, Henri thought and Give Kids the World was born.

"Each situation in life is unique," Frankl told me when we met, "and each individual ultimately someone who is irreplaceable. Each situation implies a question addressed to you and to each of us; changing from man to man and moment to moment. The world is waiting for you, waiting the day that you do something in it; that you change the situation for the better."

With characteristic, vision and persistence, Henri responded to the situation he found by beginning to cut the bureaucratic knot that kept sick children from seeing their wishes fulfilled. First, he decided to visit Dianna Morgan, then head of Disney's public relation department. What he had in mind would only work if Disney was involved.

"When I walked into her office, I had two things on my side," Henri says. "First, I had a reputation with Disney. Second, I was willing to back my proposal with money from my mother's foundation as well as from my own pocket."

As he began telling Dianna what he wanted to do, Henri realized it was something he needed to do. He had achieved success beyond anything he could have dreamed possible when he stepped off the freighter in New York twenty-five years before. His hotel business and other investments were profiting. His children were grown and healthy. But there was still something missing.

Henri knew time is the greatest enemy these children face. He vowed to do everything he could to cut through all the paperwork and red tape that wasted precious months and minutes.

"I wanted Dianna to understand the situation through my eyes," Henri says, "because my eyes were the eyes of a sick child wanting nothing more than to see Mickey Mouse."

Those who have worked with Disney know they do not lend the use of their name, characters, or company lightly. No matter how worthy the cause, every request is thoroughly vetted. So Henri fully expected it would take some time before he got an answer. To his surprise, Dianna said 'yes.' They would give him everything he asked for and more.

"I couldn't believe it," Henri says.

He was so excited that he kept asking Dianna if it was really true that Disney would support him. She told him he could count on it.

With Disney behind him, Henri knew his dream was already on the way to reality. He got in the car and drove to Sea World where he asked to meet with Sea World's President, Bob Gault.

Gault made time to see him. Quickly, Henri explained his idea. Without a moment's hesitation, Gault said, "Henri, you've got whatever you need from me."

In the months that followed, Henri was a whirlwind, going from one business to another asking them to participate. By the time he was done, over two hundred Orlando companies agreed to support him in giving kids the world. Eighty-seven hotels agreed to provide rooms when they were needed as long as there was space available.

The first year, Give Kids the World brought 380 families to Orlando for a cost-free vacation, including four nights and five days, tickets to all the theme parks, meals, and transportation. In its second year, Give Kids the World doubled in size, serving 700 families. The year after that, more than 1200 families asked for help.

Soon the demand for Give Kids the World was greater than the capacity available through local hotels. Henri realized the children needed a place of their own, a place designed with them in mind. It didn't take long for him to decide to build it.

Henri took his checkbook and began looking for a location for Give Kids the World Village. He found it almost immediately in Kissimmee. The land was located near Disney and Sea World and other major attractions. When Henri looked at the lot, he could already see the Village there. Where others might have seen rows of burned orange trees and wetlands, Henri saw villas, a place for kids to fish, and a castle.

"I could see it all," Henri says, "as if my dream had already come to life."

CHAPTER SIXTEEN

"Human beings are not fully happy or healthy

until they serve the purpose for

which God created them."

...KEN CAREY

In 1987, Henri went to San Diego for the Super Bowl. He was a guest of the Holiday Inn franchise holders. His hosts knew a little about the dream that now consumed his life. He made sure they knew everything.

Henri desperately needed help building the Village. He asked his friends for assistance. Mike Meeks, President of Holiday Inns, and Mike Rose, Holiday Inns Chairman, agreed to loan Henri the money he needed to begin. Two months later, Rose presented Henri with a check for a million dollars so construction could begin.

Henri immediately began to wonder how he could leverage Holiday Inn's contribution. He met with Gary Brown, President of Welbro Constructors, Inc., and asked him to help build the Village. Henri had worked with Welbro before and knew their values were in the right place. Gary not only agreed to build the village but also said he would help raise a million dollars of in-kind services from other builders and contractors to match Holiday Inns' money.

Now Henri had two million committed, but he knew he would need more. His business became an afterthought as he began working on his project night and day. He wanted the Village to be operational by Christmas of 1989.

Finally, Henri became so consumed with building the Village; he called his secretary and told her he would be leaving the office.

"I picked up my pen from my desk and went to the Village," Henri says. "I thought I would be gone for six to eight weeks. I never went back. That's how I finished my life as an active, participating partner in the hotel business."

With Henri's inspiration, more and more people became involved as the land was cleared and the foundations laid. Competitors worked together. Secretaries and Presidents stood side-by-side at the Village, doing whatever needed to be done. Give Kids the World had taken on a life of it's own.

One Saturday morning a group of one hundred men showed up to help. One of them pulled a set of golf clubs out of his station wagon. He took a ball out of his bag and prepared to tee off.

"What are you doing?" Henri asked.

"I've played golf every Saturday for as long as I can remember," the man replied. "I'm not going to stop now."

The volunteer hit one ball, put his clubs away, and went to work.

Eastern Airlines sent 150 employees on a Saturday to build a playground. Welbro Constructor sent 100 employees to frame the villas. Landscapers, plasterers, painters, electricians, plumbers all donated their services. One connection led to another. A volunteer who might be a plumber or painter would go home after working at the Village and talk to a friend. The next day, where there was one there would now be two. The project was contagious. Word of mouth kept the supply of labor and services flowing.

Seeing what was happening, Henri decided to feed the spirit growing at the Village and build sixteen villas instead of the eight he had originally planned. That meant he would be able to accommodate 32 families at any one time. It also meant he would need another $700,000.

Henri went back to Memphis looking for more seed money. When he found Holiday Inn could not extend its commitment, he returned home and signed a personal note guaranteeing the amount needed. Nothing could be allowed to slow down the momentum Give Kids the World Village was creating.

The first villas were finished on schedule in the winter of 1989. Construction of the administrative buildings, playground, and swimming pool were also complete when Mike Meeks, one of the project's strongest supporters at Holiday Inns, brought Donald Smith, Chairman of Perkins Family Restaurants, by the Village.

After walking through the site, Smith said, "Henri, Perkins would like to support what you are doing here. We have Friendly's Ice Cream. We can give you ice cream if you like."

Henri had barely thanked him when Smith said, "What about meals? Who is doing that?"

"No one."

"How would you like for the families to come to our restaurants and have breakfast?"

Before Henri could respond, Smith said, "No, that's not right. How about if we bring breakfast here?"

"That's even better," Henri said.

Smith stopped again. "How about this? If you get some facility built here, Perkins will come and serve breakfast and dinner."

There could be only one response. Henri said 'yes' knowing it meant he now had to build a dining facility. But what kind of facility would be appropriate?

The first thought that came to mind was a Gingerbread House. The exterior would look good enough to eat, with gingerbread walls and icing for a roof. Everything inside would be built to kid's scale. All the furniture would be made especially for them, including Plexiglas tables inlaid with real pieces of candy. Adults would only be allowed to enter at the invitation of a child.

Budget-Rent-a-Car agreed to provide seed money for The Gingerbread House. Budget had been providing transportation for the families since the beginning, now they stepped up and gave Henri $150,000 to start construction.

The Gingerbread House took six months to complete and cost over $600,000. It soon became the emotional centerpiece for the Village. As promised, Perkins provided breakfast and dinner for every family at the village, served by Perkins employees. Twenty-one years and 83,000 families later, they continue to honor their commitment.

On one of my visits to Give Kids the World, I followed Henri as he gave a tour of the Village to a group of visitors. In the middle of his presentation, Henri stopped and looked at me.

"You and I are the most selfish people I know," he said.

I remember being surprised and a little embarrassed by his remarks. I know I am not the best person in the world, but I didn't think I was that bad. Several of the people on the tour looked at me curiously. I couldn't help wondering what they were thinking.

Knowing he had our attention, Henri continued, "I know in my attempt to give back what this life has given to me, I have personally been given so much more than I have ever imagined. Much more. Most people have no idea how much we get out of what we are doing."

"Since we started Give Kids the World," he said, "I feel like somebody came along and gave me a gift—a gift of life—and that's all I want to do."

CHAPTER SEVENTEEN

"Where there is great love,

there are always miracles."

...WILLA CATHER

"If you build it, they will come," Roy Kinsella wrote in *A Field of Dreams*. The truth in his fictional baseball fantasy can be found at Give Kids the World. Every phase of building and development has been met with a greater need. Every gift has engendered a greater response.

One wish led to many. Then children from around the world began to come. The third expansion of the Village was designed to accommodate this fact with global architecture. This expansion would cost $1.5 million or about $120,000 per villa.

From the beginning, Henri's goal was to keep the Village debt free so that its existence could never be threatened. With every expansion that goal was getting harder to meet. Henri and his construction partner, Gary Brown answered the challenge by inviting every builder in town to come to the Village for a special dinner. The highlight of the evening was the presentation of their plans and a reverse auction. Each building was priced out. Instead of bidding up, builders were asked to bid down.

"Someone would say 'I'll build a villa for $100,000,'" Henri remembers with a laugh. "Then another bidder would say, 'I can do it for $90,000.' You never saw such a thing. People competing to do the work for less."

Construction at the Village was continuous for more than ten years. During that time, I visited Henri and Give Kids the World at least twice a year. Every occasion was marked by a groundbreaking or the dedication of some completed project.

Give Kids the World grew so quickly, the Village soon encompassed 70 acres. A Cupcake was added to expand the capacity of the Gingerbread house; a House of Hearts was built for reception. Then came the ice cream palace, Amberville Train Station, the Caring Center, a Chapel, and a Castle of Miracles.

A steady stream of miracles flowed through Give Kids the World development, but nothing shows God's hand at the Village more clearly than the Castle of Miracles.

"Hugh Darley, one of the owners of ITEC, came me," Henri recalls, "and said his company took on one charity project a year. He wanted it to be this castle."

A snoring tree would anchor the castle Darley described. It would rise from the center of the Village and feature a hand-carved, wooden carousel complete with wheelchair accessible figures. The inside would include interactive elements for the children, a talking wishing well, a game room, a stage, and an activity center.

"Darley said ITEC would design the castle and commit to building the interior," Henri recalls. "That alone was worth half a million dollars but as the plans developed the scope of the project grew until the budget finally reached $2.5 million."

In typical Give Kids the World fashion, Henri decided to have another auction to raise the rest. He asked ITEC to create a model of the castle, breaking the project into individual components like pieces of a puzzle. Contractors, builders, designers, suppliers, technicians, craftsmen and workers were asked to take a piece of the puzzle until each piece of the castle was adopted. Eventually, more than 300 companies participated in the project.

After committing to build the Castle, Hugh Darley sold ITEC to Bill Coan. Coan kept the verbal promise Darley had made and continued building the castle. Eighteen years later, Coan and his company are still dedicated supporters of Give Kids the World.

In all, more than 1,000 companies have helped build the Village and sustain Give Kids the World. Yet, the only names you will see there are children memorialized on buildings or street signs and stars pasted to the Castle's ceiling.

There is no accident in this. From the beginning, Henri has insisted everything be done for the children. The purity of his approach has power few would imagine. The best example is his experience with American Airlines.

In the middle of Henri's building campaign, representatives from America Airlines walked into his office and offered him a quarter of a million dollars. They said they were impressed by what Henri and his friends were doing. They said they wanted to be part of the Village, offering to construct a water park where the kids could play. The only condition was that they wanted to put their logo over the entrance.

Henri turned them down.

American Airlines' representatives were surprised and confused. To them it seemed a modest request.

Hundreds of companies had contributed to Give Kids the World, Henri explained. All together at that time they contributed more than $20 million a year in services and had helped construct a village worth more than $60 million. None of them advertised their presence or had made any effort to capitalize on their contributions.

"They all understand that everything we do here is for the kids," Henri said. "100%."

With that the American Airlines' crew left disappointed. Two weeks later they returned with a check for twice the amount they had originally offered.

They said that when they reported what happened to their Chairman, Bob Crandall, instead of greeting their report with disbelief and anger as they had expected, he responded by saying, "It's nice to know there are still some people out there with principles." Crandall told them to double American Airlines' contribution.

"For a long time I never thought that miracles existed," Henri said. "As I became involved with Give Kids the World, I am convinced that they exist in our lives. I see them almost daily. Now as I look back on my life, that's all I see—from our survival, to the Mercury years, to Give Kids the World. Miracles happen. They are real. There is no question about that. We just have to be willing to see them."

Perhaps the greatest miracle of all is that Give Kids the World Village was built without a single contract.

Today, theme park characters from all the parks visit the Village on a regular basis. Mickey and his friends visit Monday and Thursday. Sea World sends Shamu Monday for the pool party. Friday, characters from Universal visit and each Tuesday, the Royal Lipizzaner Stallions are brought for the children to ride and enjoy.

"There is no other place like this anywhere in the world," Henri says with some pride.

When he first built the Village being close to the children and their families felt painful to him. It was too close to his memories. Now he says he loves to be with them.

"When I see a child here, I don't see a calendar behind them," Henri says. "I see a living child with the rest of his or her life in front of them."

After returning from Give Kids the World last fall, a parent wrote this letter describing her experience:

"A little over 3 weeks ago, I started believing in miracles again. I had stopped believing on August 16, 2004, a day after my 38th birthday.

"It was a Monday morning, nice and warm and sunny. The day started at 6:00 am with what was supposed to be a routine hernia repair surgery for our three-year old, Mark. His brother Chris was then five and getting ready to start Kindergarten in a few weeks. Another brother was due to be born in 2 weeks. We went off to the hospital hoping to get Mark's surgery over with before the baby was born. At 11:00 AM we were sent into the black hole that every parent fears. We were told our son had cancer.

For one year straight, Mark had to receive chemotherapy every Wednesday. Every single week I would take this tiny, pale, frail little boy with sunken eyes to get what he thought was torture. I would wrap my leg around his tiny legs and hold his arms down so that the nurses could give him his chemo. He would scream and yell and try to run away. And, while every ounce in my body wanted to let him escape, I knew that doing so would lessen his chances of someday leading a normal life. Then we would go home and take care of his newborn brother and try to act like a "normal family".

No one can understand how it feels to hold down your child week after week while they struggle against you unless they have been there. Little did we know that someday we would grow from this horrible experience.

For us, the end of treatment was successful. We were some of the lucky ones. Most people around me would say — WOW it is over, you can all lead normal lives now. I thought maybe we could. But, I found that was not as easy. There were still monthly chest x-rays and ultrasounds to make sure the cancer had not recurred. I was mad and bitter. Why did we have to go through this while other kids just played and went to school? Not only does the sick child suffer but the siblings do as well. I felt cheated. What kind of world was this where children have to suffer?

Then we met some folks from Dreams Come True who sent us to Give Kids the World for Mark's wish trip to Disney World. This week long fantasy brought back all that is right with the world.

Volunteerism, America at its best, is ever present at Give Kids the World. People of all ages and backgrounds reach out to children in need to make a difference in their life. These individuals aren't getting reimbursed to be nice; they honestly care and give their love. The ability that one man had to make this his dream and the thousands of people that have made this a reality are truly inspiring.

The power of love and laughter are greater than I believed. To see these young children, all who have suffered and some who still suffer, having fun with no worries, was life changing. These families share something that we can't explain. We know what terrible road all have gone down. Yet, every family, every sibling, every wish child is having a laugh, sharing an ice cream or hugging a lovable character. It is an indescribable scene, one that I will never forget. No matter what tomorrow holds (no one knows for sure) I now know that love and kindness are the true healers.

"We cannot give to others if we do not understand what they are going through, what their needs are," Henri says. "I understand a child's pain and suffering first hand, the feeling that events are beyond control. I remember when I had no control over my life, too. I see suffering of young parents and remember the suffering of my own parents."

CHAPTER EIGHTEEN

"Love is all we have,

the only way each can help the other."

...EURIPIDES

"Any individual who survives an experience like the concentration camps," Frankl wrote in one of the last things he would send me, *"will ask himself day by day whether he has been worthy of survival, that is to say whether he has made the proper use of each and every day, and he will have to confess: only partially, if at all. Psychiatrists, particularly in your country, have come up with the concept of survivor guilt. I don't think that this concept is legitimate. I rather think that what the majority of the survivors of concentration camps experience may better be called 'survivor responsibility.' Because what we feel is a deep sense of being responsible, of having carefully to listen to what the prompter called conscience is whispering into our ears regarding the question of how to make the best of each single opportunity that life may offer us. If you put yourself in this imaged situation, you will instantaneously become conscious of the full gravity of the responsibility that every man bears throughout every*

moment of his life: the responsibility for what he will make of the next hour, for how he will shape the next day."

In 1999, Henri took inventory of his life and realized that after 15 years building Give Kids the World and the Village his work was largely done. He had created a resort like no other, a sprawling playground for terminally ill children that now rivaled the attractions they came to see, and self-sustaining charity with a multi-million dollar endowment to support its long-term operation.

"The diamond had been cut," he said. It was time to move on.

Henri moved to Ponte Vedra, Florida, a suburb of Jacksonville, to be closer to his daughter Lisa and two of his grandchildren, Sarah and Emily. Five weeks after he had settled in, he realized he was bored. He was used to making things happen, a phone that never stopped ringing, and meetings without end. Now, he didn't know what to do with himself.

Lisa and Hugh Jones, a friend of long-standing, encouraged him to visit Jacksonville's homeless shelter, the I. M. Sulzbacher Center. Hugh had championed the building of a homeless shelter while President of Barnett Banks in Jacksonville. Lisa was intimately aware of its operation through her work in Jacksonville on behalf of the Fanny Landwirth Foundation.

Lisa and Hugh thought the Sultzbacher Center would interest Henri because of his experiences after the war. They knew he had wandered through Czechoslovakia and Germany for months, as homeless and disturbed as the people on the streets of Jacksonville, foraging for food in garbage cans, stealing clothes, and sleeping where he could.

"I stole clothes to get out of the concentration camp uniform," Henri recalls, describing those days. "I stole shoes to protect my feet. I had no underwear or socks. I was hungry, sick, and out of my head."

Almost as soon as he arrived at the Sulzbacher Center, Henri found himself offering to help. "What do you need?" he asked one of the residents. There was no response. He repeated his question again. Still no response. Finally, he told them he too had been homeless and that he knew what their lives were like. Almost immediately, everyone started talking.

"We need to get out of here," one man said.

"I want to find a place to live," another responded.

Henri said he really couldn't help with that. What else did they need?

A middle-aged man, skin hanging loosely on his bones from years of malnutrition and being on the streets, stood up. With what was left of his dignity, he pulled down his pants to reveal his naked buttocks.

"I need some underwear," he said.

"That's something I can help you with," Henri said, and Dignity U Wear was born.

Before he had returned home, Henri was back in action. He began by calling all the corporate contacts in his network. He asked his friends at K-Mart if he could buy all the packages of underwear and socks that had been opened by customers or returned to the store. K-Mart quickly agreed. Sears offered to give him surplus children's clothing if he promised not to resell it. Henri accepted their offer, even though he didn't have any recipients in mind at the time.

Within months, the Sulzbacher Center overflowed with new underwear and socks. What Sulzbacher couldn't use immediately was stored in rented storage units whose number seemed to increase each month. Soon Henri realized Dignity U Wear needed its own warehouse.

He found a warehouse on Myrtle Avenue that had been empty for seven years. It was cold and uninviting, but Henri knew he could make it work. He agreed to purchase the building, offering to pay $200,000 for the property before he knew where the money would come from.

Several days later, a letter from the MIKI Corporation arrived at Henri's house. MIKI offered him $200,000 to come to Japan and speak to their employees.

Henri believes the timing was more than coincidental. He had never before been offered an honorarium of that size. It was one more of the many miracles he has come to see in his life.

When he returned from Japan, Henri met with Jay Stein, Chairman of the Board of Stein Mart. Stein Mart, based in Jacksonville, had supported Dignity from its inception. Now Henri asked Jay to help him find a way to cut through the retail process and get manufactures involved. Without hesitation, Jay agreed, telling his buyers to call the manufacturers they worked with and ask them to send Dignity their overruns and any other clothing they could not use.

Over night with Jay's help, a pipeline to the manufacturers—Izod, Rafael, Levi-Straus, Sears, Limited Brands, and many more—had been created. Clothes began pouring in— more than could be distributed locally in the Jacksonville community.

Since Stein Mart had helped create this wonderful new problem, it seemed logical they should help solve it. Henri met with Michael Fisher, President and CEO of Stein Mart and suggested they partner in expanding operations to other communities and other states. The partnership they created now involves some 20,000 Stein Mart associates and 282 stores nationwide. Stein Mart associates choose local beneficiaries and help raise the money to support Dignity U Wear's mission of providing the needy and their families with clothing for "A Brand New Life."

Between 2000 and 2005, Dignity delivered 1 million pieces of clothing to children and families in need. That total was doubled the following year. To date, Dignity has delivered more than 2 million pieces of clothing worth more than $33 million to 200,000 people in need, including over 100,000 children. What began as a small local diversion to occupy Henri's idle time now serves 260 agencies in 31 states.

With Give Kids the World and Dignity U Wear Henri had addressed the needs he felt as a child during the holocaust and as a survivor after the war. Now, still in need of something to do, he focused on the memories of love he had for his parents.

He knew from his experience at Give Kids the World that there were as many families troubled by the possible loss of a parent as there were families facing the possible loss of a child. He had been a child facing death. He knew how difficult it was to lose a parent.

"At the end of life all we have left is memories," Henri said. He decided to focus on giving troubled families facing the loss of a parent a happy time they could always cherish—memories of love.

The Memories of Love Foundation was established in August of 2005. It is the obverse of Give Kids the World, focusing on the illness of a parent rather than a child, but its purpose and the experience are essentially the same – giving troubled families a cost-free vacation in Orlando, days off from disease, and what may be their last joyful time together as a family.

Memories of Love was co-founded by Mel Gottlieb, a good friend who tragically lost his son from complications due to surgery in 2004.

"I know from experience," Mel says, "you really remember those last months. We want that time to be as happy as possible for the families we serve."

CHAPTER NINETEEN

"We must learn to love each other or die."

...W. H. AUDEN

For years Henri did not want to remember the holocaust. Now he spends much of his time trying to make sure others will never forget.

"Many people do not believe the Holocaust happened," Henri says. "I wish I could sit and talk with them one at a time. I would explain the Holocaust can happen again if they turn away from the lessons of the past."

Henri's concern is fueled by awareness that the forces of darkness are persistent and always on the present.

On August 22, 1939, Hitler told his Army commanders, "I have sent to the East only my 'Death's Head Units' with the orders to kill without pity or mercy all men, women, and children of Polish race or language. Only in such a way will we win the vital space that we need." Hitler concluded by asking the rhetorical question, "Who still talks nowadays about the

Armenians?" He was referring to the destruction of 1.5 million Armenians in Turkey between 1915 and 1918.

It was the first of many genocides and other crimes against humanity that paraded through the 20th Century seemingly without end: In 1932 and 1933 in what has been called the forgotten holocaust, Joseph Stalin, then leader of the Soviet Union, murdered more than 7 million people – a quarter of the Ukraine's population. Over 3 million of his victims were children. After World War II, the world said "never again", yet Pol Pot, the former leader of the Khymer Rouge, killed two million people in Cambodia. Ethnic and religious differences resulted in the death of more than 200,000 people in Bosnia. In 1994, somewhere between 800,000 and 1,000,000 people were killed in 100 days in the Rwandan. Since February 2003, the Sudanese government in Khartoum and the government-sponsored Janjaweed militia has used rape, organized starvation, and mass murder to kill more than 400,000 and displace 2.5 million people in Darfur, an area about the size of Texas. While the number has not been tallied, scarcely a day has gone by in the last thirty years without an act of violence in the Middle East.

Hoping to make a point, I helped to bring a matched pair of children from the Middle East to Give Kids the World in 1996. Eight-year-old, Maataz Kishta came from Palestine. Nine-year-old Chiam Salinas was from Israel.

Both boys were fighting cancer. Both had under gone a bone marrow transfer. Both faced long odds and were hoping for a miracle.

I met them at the airport in New York City. Almost by design, they seemed to come from different ends of the plane. Chiam arrived first, Maataz a few minutes later. They took positions on opposite sides of me while my translator helped me greet them and their escorts.

While we waited for the plane to Orlando, they kept as much distance between themselves as possible. Both wanted to know what we had planned for them, but each asked their questions independently. There was no direct communication. They could not avoid being close from time to time, but there was no connection between them.

A week later, after meeting Henri, playing together, eating together, sharing rides, and experiencing the wonders of Orlando's theme parks, they left as friends. Somehow along the way, they learned they had more than a disease and a desire to meet Mickey Mouse in common.

"This is the most beautiful thing," Maataz' father, Aatef, told Antonio Mora of ABC News as they were leaving.

Chiam's mother, Shula, agreed. "We hope people can learn from this" she said. "I know I have."

In 2001 with a growing awareness of the need to combat the rising tide of hate, Henri did something he thought he would never do again: He returned to Poland. Margot, his wife, Linda, two of his children, Gary and Lisa, and a film crew preparing a documentary on his life accompanied him. For more than 3 years, the film crew had followed Henri around, filming various aspects of his life. Now they wanted to see where it began—and nearly ended.

The film, *Borrowing Time*, moves from the sunlight of his current life to the darkness of his past, juxtaposing images of joy – his family, children laughing, and Give Kids the World— with stark images of Auschwitz, Mauthausen, and the Krakow Ghetto.

One of the more compelling scenes finds Henri standing at the junction of the railway tracks in the switching yard at Auschwitz.

"This is where my destiny was decided," he tells his children. "I remember it like yesterday. We were separated right here. So much commotion. People running in many directions. Those who could work on one side. Those who could not on the other."

The camera pans to a sign posted in German over the camps entrance. "Work Makes You Free," Henri translates. "Lies. Nothing but Lies."

"I tried to hide pictures of my mother and father but there was no way to hide anything," Henri tells Lisa. "They took them away from me. They took our clothes, cut our hair, and gave us uniforms. We didn't know what was going to happen to us when we were here."

Next the scene shifts to the last apartment he had shared with his family. It is no longer a ghetto, but the curfews and ghetto memories live on in Henri's mind.

"This is where we were forced to live. More than once I had to stay outside and watch them hanging people who tried to run a way. We couldn't be on the street after 9:00 PM."

Another family lives there now. After an explanation and some persuasion, Henri and his crew are allowed to enter and look around. As he walks up the stairs, Henri becomes increasingly anxious. He cannot enter what was his parent's room. Choked with emotion, he apologizes and hurriedly leaves.

Two days later, Henri had a stroke. He had gone to Rome after shooting wrapped up in Poland. In the middle of the night he woke to find the room was spinning. He could not see or stand.

Fortunately, Linda recognized the symptoms and called an ambulance to take him to the hospital. He made a full recovery, but the incident reinforced his sense of mortality and heightened his resolve to make sure people understand what hate can do.

For most of his life, Henri had avoided talking about his childhood experiences. His children knew he had survived the holocaust but he never told what he had gone through in the camps until they were grown with families of their own. There are still many places he still cannot go, memories too painful to share.

So completely has Henri avoided talking about his experiences in the camps that he only recently learned the details of his mother's death. Henri had long known where and when his mother died, but he had never known until it was revealed in a casual conversation with Margot last year how his Mother was lost.

Fanny and Margot were together throughout the entire war until one fateful moment in Auschwitz when Margot went to the restroom. When Margot returned, Fanny was gone. A cruel twist of fate in an instant defined life or death for the two people Henri loved most in the world, sparing one while taking the other.

"Decent people, really human people, we may say, form a minority," Viktor said. *"But isn't this minority exactly what constitutes a challenge to ourselves? The challenge to follow them, to*

join them. This is why we have to feel the responsibility to do something. Our generation now knows—the generation I mean after Auschwitz, after Dachau, after Treblinka, after Mauthausen—what man is capable of. Man is the individual who has invented gas chambers to be sure but he is also the individual who has entered these very gas chambers, head held high and with dignity. In addition, we are not only living in a time where we have got to know what man is capable of, but also at the time where we know after Hiroshima what is at stake. So we have to be alert, we have to do our best, whatever we can, each of us, we have to meet our responsibilities. An education should not only be education toward knowledge but also an education toward refining young people's conscience, conscience as I have said before is the prompter who gives us a vision of what can be done and what should be done."

Henri has always had an innate sense of what can be done. The tragic death of a fifteen-year old boy at a high school near his home in March of 2006 made him wonder what more he could do to fight the forces of darkness.

The boy had committed suicide. While no one knows for sure why this child chose to end his life, racism was believed to be a contributing factor. A black boy in a predominately white rural school, he was constantly subjected to racial slurs and mocked by his peers.

After the boy's death, the school was rocked by a series of race related incidents. Concerned about the escalating violence, the principal invited Henri to speak to the student body, hoping his story might cause students to think about the consequences of their actions.

Henri told them how hate had nearly destroyed his life. He talked about the five years of torture and brutality he had endured at their age, his desire for vengeance, and the miracles that followed his forgiveness. He urged the students to make love not hate the focus of their lives. And he asked them to practice forgiveness.

"If you cannot forgive, you cannot love fully," he said, "and life without love is nothing."

The following day, an English teacher at the school gave her students a pop quiz. "I have never done anything like that following an assembly," she said, "but there has never been an assembly like that one."

To her surprise nearly every student made eighty percent or above on the quiz. Inspired by the student's response, Henri cancelled plans for a vacation and began seeking engagements at local high schools, hoping to teach tolerance, forgiveness, and compassion.

In the summer of 2006 as part of this effort, Henri, gathered his children and grandchildren, proof of the failure of Hitler's grand design, to do what he had not done before and talk about the holocaust.

Henri's children, Gary, Greg, and Lisa, have all followed his example. Each is a success in their own right and each has created a charity of their own. The four grandchildren range in age from twelve to fifteen.

Turning to his grandson, Henri said, "Max, I was your age when I was taken to a camp."

That simple statement brings Henri's experience into their reality. It takes a moment for Max to process his grandfather's statement. He is thirteen going on twenty, fun loving and focused. The thought of being in a concentration camp is hard for him to imagine.

"What was the hardest part of that experience?" he asks.

"I say the hunger was the worst. I was all by myself. I saw all my friends die around me. You never know what they are going to do to you, where you are going. It was very difficult. But the hunger is more than anything you can imagine. It's just torture by itself."

Sarah is fifteen and thinks with her heart. She has just returned from a mission trip to Mississippi.

"How did your experience in the camps influence who you are today?" she asks.

"I live my life to the fullest because I know I live on borrowed time," Henri answers. "I cherish my life. And it is extremely important for me to help other people because of what I went through. It's almost like a gift from God that I have been able to do all this."

Rebecca at the age of fifteen is already thinking of a career in communications. Going for the bottom line, she asks the reporter's question.

"Why do you think it is so important for us to know about the Holocaust?" she says.

"Those of us who lived through the Holocaust are a dying generation. I am one of the youngest survivors," Henri responds. "We said never again, yet I look around and see the same thing happening all around the world. We cannot go on this way; the world cannot exist with so much hate. It is extremely important that we have a mutual understanding for each other and even more important for us all to love each other."

Emily is twelve years old, the youngest. "They killed your mother and father," she says. "If you hadn't survived we wouldn't be here. How could you forgive the Germans?"

"I had to," Henri says. "I couldn't live any other way. The lesson we must learn from the Holocaust is that evil is real. It has existed since the inception of man, and will continue until mankind is extinct. That is why we must talk about what happened in the concentration camps. People have to understand where hatred leads."

"The greatest challenge of the day is how to bring about

a revolution of the heart, a revolution

which has to start with

each one of us."

...DOROTHY DAY

When I first met Dr. Frankl, I asked him about forgiveness.

"People ask me time and again why I returned to Vienna after the war," Viktor responded. 'Have they done too little to you and your family?' they would say. 'Your mother died in the gas chambers of Auschwitz. Your father died in Treblinka. Your brother died in a coal mine in Auschwitz. Your first wife died in Bergen-Belsen. Is it too little they have done to you?'"

"And I answer, what have they done to me?"

"There is no collective guilt. This is a lie. There is only personal guilt. You can hold someone responsible only for what he has done personally, or has omitted to do personally. But you cannot condemn *him for something that a population has done and least of all can you condemn him for what his ancestors have done or omitted to do. This is absolute nonsense. It was the experience of Jews in Europe throughout the Hitler regime. Is this lesson too little a lesson?*

"Everywhere this can happen. Everywhere. Anti-Semitism, nationalism, chauvinism, concentration camps, holocausts for that matter, is not a monopoly of the German population. In each country this can happen again and again."

On March 10, 2007, friends and family from around the world gather to mark Henri's 80th birthday. Heads and former heads of Disney, Universal, SeaWorld, and Nickelodeon, astronauts and former astronauts, executives from Holiday Inns and other business partners, as well as the leaders and supporters of the various charities Henri has created are present to help celebrate the gift of his life.

Rather than stop and enjoy what he has done, however, Henri's mind is focused on what he is now trying to do. The effort he began with local school children and his grandchildren six months before has flowered into yet another foundation – The Gift of Life in America – and a new program: Hate Hurts.

Henri has returned to where he began. He returns with the knowledge that this is the battle of his lifetime. Everything he has done seems to have prepared him for what he is now doing. In truth, his entire life has been an attempt to answer hate with love. He is now looking for schools to visit every week, talking with students about the Holocaust.

Before the party, Henri convenes a meeting to talk about his new program. My wife Angie and I are among the handful of people in the room. In a few minutes Henri describes the elements of the campaign he is organizing—a website, traveling exhibits, and personal appearances designed to teach tolerance, understanding, and compassion.

A student group called HYPE (Helping You Pursue Equality) has been formed at Jacksonville's Community College to support this effort. The group has designed pledge cards they plan to distribute to the 60,000 students at the college asking them to make a personal commitment to tolerance, equality, and diversity.

This effort has the full support of Steven Wallace, President of the College, who hopes the seeds being spread on his campus will spread to other colleges and universities.

"Henri is the best living example of the lessons of the Holocaust," he says. "I want to help him tell his compelling and inspirational story to as broad an audience as possible."

Like everyone else present, Angie and I are quick to endorse

Henri's vision and pledge our support. Though everyone in the room has known Henri for some time, it is still hard to believe how much he has done in such a short period of time.

After listening to our reactions, Henri turned to address one of those in the room directly. He is Mark Snyder, Vice President for Brand Management of Holiday Inns and Holiday Inns Express.

"Do you know why you are here now?" Henri asks.

Everyone including Mark laughs, knowing what is coming.

"I want Holiday Inns to support this program."

I expected a political response, something to the effect that he liked the idea but would have to run it by the boys in Atlanta. To my surprise, Mark is quick to agree. Quicker than I would have thought possible, he pledges Holiday Inns and Holiday Inns Express support at their 3,500 locations world wide.

I can't help shaking my head in wonder. When we arrived, Henri had an embryonic local program. The ink was barely dry on the papers giving his new charity IRS approval. Within minutes, he has gone global.

Noting my reaction, Henri pulls me aside as we leave the room.

"How's that for an ending to your book?" he says.

"You can't solve a problem on the same level as it was created. You have to rise above it to the next level."

… ALBERT EINSTEIN

Dreams come true. Nightmares end.

In April 2000, the Heart of America organized an event to commemorate the first anniversary of the tragedy at Columbine High School. As it happened, I had been in Denver the year before for a speaking engagement at the Denver College of Law. After my presentation, a couple of students asked if we could get together that night and talk about what had happened.

That evening six of us met for pizza at a little restaurant near the campus. For more than an hour, I listened as the students talked about the shootings, how terrible it was and who was responsible. Some blamed the shooters and their parents. Others blamed the principal, the school board, the sheriff's office, and others in positions of authority.

Finally, when they had expressed their feelings and frustrations, I asked the question Viktor taught me: What are you going to do about it? Forget what anyone else can do, may do, or might not do, what can *we* do to make things better?

With that, the entire character of the conversation changed. Ideas started flying, one building on another until "A Day of Hope" emerged. By the time I left Denver two days later, over 200 students were involved in the process.

The concept these students came up with was to encourage other concerned students to be the change they wanted to see in the world, to answer the negative with the positive and counter hate with love. As part of this effort, The Heart of America's Foundation agreed to fly sixty of its national youth Ambassadors in for the occasion. We also invited Henri, one of the Heart of America's founding board members, to keynote a student rally and launch the day's activities.

When Henri concluded his remarks, Pat Ireland came forward. Pat Ireland had been shot three times at Columbine, including once in the head. His dramatic fall from the library into the arms of waiting SWAT teams created the most memorable image of that tragic event.

For a year, Pat had been silent. He refused to speak to the media and would not discuss what happened even with his friends. After hearing what Henri had to say, Pat quietly began to tell his own story. Like Henri, he said, what he had gone through had taught him something about the nature of love and hate, the meaning of courage, and the preciousness of life. Pat asked people to remember those who lost their lives a year before and those who were injured, but to also take a moment to think about their own responsibility.

"The battle against hate begins with simple acts of kindness," he said, "knowing people's names and speaking to everyone. Making a point to just be nice to people."

After the rally, HOA's Ambassadors fanned out to speak at schools across the Denver area and spread the word. They were able to reach some 10,000 students in that one day with their positive message of hope and responsibility.

That evening, Henri helped host a dinner and celebration. As the dinner concluded, Henri stood to applaud the Ambassadors' efforts and offer a toast.

"There are a lot of things the world needs but what we most need is the love you have to give," he said. "Never forget that."

When Frankl was Henri's age, I asked him how he wanted to be remembered. "When I started my professional life," he said, "I had three wishes. I wanted to become a psychiatrist. I became a psychiatrist. I wanted to become a good psychiatrist. I hope I was not one of the worst psychiatrist. And the third wish was I wanted to remain a human being. I am still wrestling with this wish to fulfill."

Asked how he would like to be remembered more than a dozen years later, Henri's responded in much the same manner.

"I would like to be remembered as having contributed something in this little world of ours," he said. "I would like to be remembered as a good person. I'd like to be remembered as someone who had a positive influence on at least some human beings around the world."

To paraphrase Andre Gide, everything has been said but since no one listens we must always begin again. Henri's secret is as old as time. It is a lesson we have long been taught but yet to fully learn. From generation to generation, Moses to Mohammed, Jesus to Buddha, Ghandi, King, Mandela and the rest, we have been reminded: We are here to love one another.

When hate is used to combat hate, hate wins. Revenge brings retribution and the mentality of an eye-for-an-eye leaves everyone blind. The only way out of this descending spiral is to rise above and seek higher ground.

This is the great lesson of Henri's life. No matter what the problem is the answer will always be found when we surround it with love. It is in loving and giving that we find meaning and purpose for our lives.

About The Cover

Yousuf Karsh is recognized as the premier portrait photographer of the 20th century. He was born in Armenia in 1908, leaving for the New World at the age of sixteen. Shortly after arriving in Canada, he was sent to Boston to study with the portrait photographer, John H. Garo.

"Garo taught me more than technique," Karsh said; "he taught me to see and remember what I saw. You have to understand what you are seeking to achieve and when it is there, record it. Art is never fortuitous."

After three years under Garo, Karsh returned to Canada to open his own studio. He achieved some success almost immediately, photographing prominent local businessmen and political figures. Then in 1941 came the moment that changed his life. Learning that Winston Churchill would visit Ottawa in late December as part of his effort to mobilize North American governments against Nazi Germany, Karsh asked for an opportunity to photograph the Prime Minister while he was there. After pleading his case for months, the Canadian authorities finally agreed to grant the young photographer's request. But he was told he would only have a few minutes and he would have set up in one of the Canadian Parliament's corridors so that he could catch Churchill between meetings.

What Karsh was not told was that Churchill was unaware of the appointment and, as a result, so irritated that he was uncooperative, refusing to take the cigar from his mouth long enough for a suitable portrait. Seizing the moment, Karsh plucked the cigar from his mouth, capturing Churchill's defiant and belligerent reaction. Within months, Karsh's photograph was being celebrated as the defining image of the British Empire's resistance to Nazi Germany.

"My portrait of Winston Churchill opened the doors of the world to me and started me on my search for greatness," Karsh would later say. "The endless fascination of these people for me lies in what I call their inward power."

In the fifty years that followed, Karsh photographed the most significant figures of his time, seeking to reveal that inward power. "The heart and mind are the true lens of the camera," he said. The moment I want to record is when the mask is down and people reveal who they really are."

In the spring of 1992, Henri and I traveled to Ottawa to visit Karsh. I had met Karsh several years before as part of my own search for greatness and we became friends. As a present for Henri's 65th birthday, I asked him if he would take Henri's portrait.

When Karsh heard Henri's story, he quickly agreed. He too had experienced love and hate, finding a new life in the New World after surviving Turkish atrocities against the Armenians. After seven years of genocide, Karsh's family was allowed to flee, their lives their only baggage.

Repeatedly through the years of our friendship, Karsh had told me of the ruthless and hideous persecution that formed his earliest memories. Particularly he remembered the terrifying ordeal of sneaking food passed armed guards in the night to help keep alive two uncles who had been thrown into a well to perish.

The evening we arrived in Ottawa, Henri and I dined with Yousuf and his charming wife, Estralita. To all appearances it was a social event but in truth the artist was at work, forming the impression he hoped to capture the next day.

In the morning we met in Karsh's studio, walking past floor to ceiling enlargements, larger than life portraits of some of the larger than life figures of our time—Ernest Hemingway, Helen Keller, Albert Schweitzer, Albert Einstein, and a few of Karsh's other favorites—to a surprisingly simple set: two lights, a box camera with a cable release, some drapery, and a chair.

Karsh asked Henri to sit and face the camera. The two talked for a few minutes while Karsh put Henri at ease. He snapped the shutter when he saw his moment, capturing the strength, courage, great sadness and wells of compassion in Henri's face.

Two weeks later, in June of 1992 Karsh closed his studio and formally retired.